THE LAZARUS LIFE

"The Lazarus Life *is a radiantly hopeful book about the promise of resurrection in the places where we are most dead. Enter into the Lazarus story and say yes to Jesus' invitation to 'Come forth' and live!*"
—Ruth Haley Barton, cofounder and president of The Transforming Center and author of *Invitation to Solitude and Silence, Sacred Rhythms,* and *Strengthening the Soul of Your Leadership*

"*Steve Smith has given us a delightful and very readable tour of the subject of the truly converted Christian life. Some might call it life renovation.* The Lazarus Life *is a book for any man or woman who believes that one should keep on keeping on—loosed from the past, confident of the future, growing in the present.*"
—Gordon MacDonald, author and pastor

"*This book is a resource whose time has come. Steve Smith has written a vulnerable, practical, true-companion guide to finding an identity rooted in the love of Christ. You will return to this book again and again.*"
—Paula Rinehart, author of *Strong Women, Soft Hearts* and *Better Than My Dreams*

"*With simplicity and integrity, Steve Smith offers his keen insights taken from the Lazarus story. In so doing, he tells my story of desperate yearning for deep and lasting change. To the soul-sick who are looking for a certain cure, I pray that this book will bring hope and healing to your soul in the profound way that it has renewed mine.*"
—Fil Anderson, author of *Running on Empty*

"*Steve Smith has plumbed the depths of three things—his own life, the life of ordinary men and women he's met, and especially the life of Lazarus, 'whom Jesus raised from the dead.' As these lives all converge, a wondrous thing happens: Lazarus becomes freshly alive before us and we feel the stirrings of new life within us. And then, more: the voice of Jesus breaks through the stone of our own tomb, our own heart, and bids us, 'Come forth!' This is a book that will allow you to experience personally, deeply, maybe for the first time, Jesus' love for you, His miracle with you. It's a book that will give you hope.*"
—Mark Buchanan, pastor and author of *Hidden in Plain Sight* and *Your God Is Too Safe*

"*Steve Smith has unpacked the story of Lazarus's resurrection as a lens through which we can see the multifaceted dynamics of the spiritual journey out of our deadness into resurrection life. This is one of the most balanced and thorough portrayals of spiritual transformation I have read. This is a must read for anyone engaged in mentoring others on the spiritual journey and a welcome guide for those on the journey.*"

—Dr. M. Robert Mulholland Jr., author of *Invitation to a Journey* and *The Deeper Journey*

"*Stephen W. Smith is not afraid to tackle one of the most intimidating questions: Why is God so silent when we most need His presence? With much experience and wisdom, Smith walks us through the journey of real transformation, as we learn to see God with new eyes, through our suffering and waiting. There is, indeed, purpose in our pain! We have much to learn about our own life as we experience a fresh encounter with the remarkable story of Lazarus and his mysterious friend Jesus.*"

—Charlie Lowell, Jars of Clay

"*In* The Lazarus Life, *the voice of Jesus calls through the words of Steve Smith, 'Come forth!' Steve then becomes one of those servants whom God uses to gently, but firmly unwrap our graveclothes, allowing us to live in the freedom for which Christ has set us free. I am thrilled that* The Lazarus Life *is available to do for its readers what the ministry of its author has done for me.*"

—Howard Baker, instructor of Christian Formation, campus chaplain at Denver Seminary, and author of *Soul Keeping* and *The One True Thing*

THE LAZARUS
LIFE

STEPHEN W. SMITH

THE LAZARUS
LIFE

spiritual transformation
for ordinary people

David C Cook
transforming lives together

THE LAZARUS LIFE
Published by David C. Cook
4050 Lee Vance View
Colorado Springs, CO 80918 U.S.A.

David C. Cook Distribution Canada
55 Woodslee Avenue, Paris, Ontario, Canada N3L 3E5

David C. Cook U.K., Kingsway Communications
Eastbourne, East Sussex BN23 6NT, England

David C. Cook and the graphic circle C logo
are registered trademarks of Cook Communications Ministries.

The Web site addresses recommended throughout this book are offered as a resource
to you. These Web sites are not intended in any way to be or imply an endorsement
on the part of David C. Cook, nor do we vouch for their content.

All Scripture quotations, unless otherwise noted, are taken from the *Holy Bible, New
International Version*®. *NIV*®. Copyright © 1973, 1978, 1984 by International Bible Society.
Used by permission of Zondervan. All rights reserved. Scripture quotations marked MSG are
taken from *THE MESSAGE*. Copyright © by Eugene H. Peterson 1993, 1994, 1995, 1996,
2000, 2001, 2002. Used by permission of NavPress Publishing Group. Scripture quotations
marked NLT are taken from the *Holy Bible, New Living Translation*, copyright © 1996. Used
by permission of Tyndale House Publisher, Inc., Wheaton, Illinois 60189. All rights reserved.
Scripture quotations marked AB are taken from *The Amplified Bible*. Copyright © 1954, 1958,
1962, 1964, 1965, 1987 by The Lockman Foundation. Used by permission.
Italics in Scripture are added by the author for emphasis.

LCCN 2008924983
ISBN 978-1-4347-9995-1

The Team: John Blase, Amy Kiechlen, and Jaci Schneider
Cover Design: Studiogearbox, Chris Gilbert
Interior Design: The DesignWorks Group

Printed in the United States of America
First Edition 2008

1 2 3 4 5 6 7 8 9 10

032708

THE LAZARUS LIFE

is dedicated to

Lazarus of Bethany, first century AD,

Giotto di Bondone, fourteenth century AD,

and

Dallas Willard, twenty-first century AD,

CONTENTS

ACKNOWLEDGMENTS

Writing an ordinary book on such an extraordinary subject has been its own unparalleled journey for me. It's been exhilarating and exhausting. I have known about Lazarus for many years, as you may have as well. But it was not until I was thumbing through an art book that I saw, as if for the first time, more than I had ever seen before from John's account in his gospel. Page after page of art revealed Lazarus emerging from the tomb. Primitive, medieval, Renaissance, and modern artists all tried to convey on canvas what John was saying in his gospel. Each painting tells a different part of the story but all say the same thing—the Lazarus life is possible!

Together, the paintings and gospel made for me a sort of movie to look at anytime I wanted or needed. I began to see myself in the paintings, especially the one featured in this book by Giotto di Bondone. Giotto is recognized as a pioneer of sorts because he was among the first of the Italian painters to offer mood, expressions, and emotions in his paintings. He is widely recognized to be an important figure in the Italian Renaissance painting movement. As Giotto painted the Lazarus story, some of the observers have halos; some do not. Some are recoiling from Lazarus; some are touching him. Some are worshipping, and some are doubting. Lazarus is present, of course, but barely alive and fully wrapped in the dreadful graveclothes. It's as if Giotto was determined to put each of us there—right in the middle of the story—standing with Jesus and Lazarus at some unique stage of our spiritual journey.

I don't think I will ever be "done" with Lazarus. I hope you won't either. As I discovered some of the insights Lazarus offers us, I began to give talks, preach sermons, and use Lazarus as a tool to help people understand how transformation actually happens. The results were almost always so encouraging that I began to realize something was "up" that I needed to pay attention to and develop more. I am indebted to each artist who painted and each writer who ever penned a word about this amazing man named Lazarus. Each of you has helped me in such a significant way.

I had the privilege of working with several publishers to decide the best fit for *The Lazarus Life*. In the end I chose David C. Cook to publish this book, and I'm very glad I did. David C. Cook itself is transforming and has adopted the tagline of "Transforming Lives Together," which you will see on the back cover of this book. I was particularly interested in David C. Cook because of its commitment to the local church—a place I have lived and spent all of my working life trying to help. My deepest thanks to the David C. Cook team for believing in this project and for offering me John Blase as my editor, who crafted the words when I was stuck or afraid and polished all the others. You dreamed the dream with me, and together we see more than a book emerging between the two of us. Special thanks to Elisa Fryling Stanford, who spent hours with me developing the chapters, filling in missing pieces, and enlarging my own understanding of *The Lazarus Life*. We both recognized that *The Lazarus Life* seemed to take on a life that was bigger, deeper, and wider than words typed on a computer or printed on a page. May it be so!

Throughout the writing of this book, dear friends have stood with me who not only know about transformation but who for me are trophies of transformation. Among you are: Rick Campbell, John and Denise Kapitan, Chuck and Kim Millsap, Sean and Kathy Buchanan, Lea and Susie Courtney, Russell and Kate Courtney, Jim and Renee Hughes, Frank Rudy, Bob and Sherry Sprotte, Jim and Leta Van Meter, Scott and Beth Shaum, and Greg and Yvonne Meyer.

I am deeply indebted to the supporters of the Potter's Inn ministry. You faithfully stand with us and generously support the ongoing ministry of our retreats, soul care, and the development of resources such as this important one.

The stories in this book are all true, but the names have been changed to protect the guilty and the transformed! Each person who has sat with me and talked with me has in fact become a mentor to help me to understand the lingering Jesus, the smelly graveclothes, and the ongoing miracle of transformation more deeply. Thank you. Special thanks to the readers who not only read the manuscript, but offered insight into how to strengthen it.

Along my own journey of transformation, I have found companions—some literary and some in the flesh—who have walked with me and who took hold of my own graveclothes and pushed me forward to Jesus. You are Craig and Beryl Glass, Paula Rinehart, Dallas Willard, David Benner, Henri Nouwen, Ray and Lynn Walkowski, Michael and Hallie Doyle, Gloria Smith Schwartz (my beloved sister), Gwen H. Smith (my very beloved wife), and Blake, Jordan, Cameron, and Leighton Smith (my very beloved sons).

I also thank my parents, Sonny and Rena Smith, for helping me understand my deepest desire and my most profound need—to experience authentic transformation.

Stephen W. Smith
Potter's Inn at Aspen Ridge
Divide, Colorado

I AM LAZARUS:

FINDING OURSELVES IN THE STORY

Now a man named Lazarus was sick.
He was from Bethany ...

—as told by John, the beloved disciple in John 11:1

- We are all soul-sick and in need of transformation.
- Transformation does not come from earning love. It comes from being loved.
- Only Jesus offers us the life we long for.
- The story of Lazarus is the story of the Christian life.

am Lazarus. And I believe you are too. His story is our story. I'd like to invite you to come with me into this story, a story that I trust you'll come to see as your own, as I've come to see it as mine. It is the ongoing story of someone who is experiencing transformation. Someone who needs a miracle to be whole.

The Lazarus Life is the story of our longing for deep and lasting change. But it is more than that—much more than that. The story is an invitation to live, but this invitation will prove to be like none you've ever received before.

As we accept this invitation, we'll see Lazarus getting weaker and more desperate for healing, asking us to evaluate our own spiritual condition. When all the efforts of friends and relatives fail to persuade Jesus to show up and fix the situation, we'll be invited to explore the hidden resentments held in our own hearts about a Jesus who doesn't always show up on time—and about our own community of well-intentioned family and friends who often fail us. When Lazarus dies and is placed in a tomb, an invitation will surface to peer into the dark places in our own lives, the dark places that keep us buried when we long for new life. When Lazarus hears a voice—not just any voice, but the voice of Jesus—we, too, can learn how to listen for that same voice today when it calls us to move forward. As Lazarus gets "unraveled" from his situation, we can become unstuck from our own, even if it's a messy process. When Lazarus emerges from the tomb trapped in graveclothes, we'll examine the "graveclothes" of our lives—such as self-rejection, fear, sin, guilt, blame and shame, and disappointment—that hold us back from renewed spiritual vigor. And when Lazarus steps into his new, resurrected life, we will see a hint of the life that Jesus invites us to today—the dangerous, rewarding, radical, powerful life of transformation.

The story of Lazarus is about longings and breakthroughs. It is about unmet expectations and disillusionment with God. It is about overcoming obstacles. It is about facing our disappointments so that we can move forward. It is about freedom and life. Yes—life! The life that Jesus described when He said, "I have come that they may have life, and have it to the full" (John 10:10). Maybe we're burned out in ministry, work, family, or all of the above. Maybe we're tired of waiting for the circumstances of our lives to change. Maybe we find ourselves buried in a tomb, overwhelmed with both past and future, yet God is calling us forth to something that "may be"—to a better life than we ever dreamed.[1]

LOOKING FOR SOMETHING MORE

We're not the first people to be moved toward abundant life through Lazarus's story. Buried under the sprawling city of Rome are darkened catacombs, the place of burial for early believers. Many of these early Christians were persecuted, terrorized, and ill-treated. Yet the story of Lazarus so inspired these Christians that ordinary people—not theologians, priests, or popes—painted artistic renditions on frescoes that we can still see today. In fact more than sixty renditions of the raising of Lazarus can be found etched and painted on the dark walls of the tunnels that lead to the burial sites. Those ancient limestone walls reveal images of Jesus Christ at an opened tomb from which a bound, mummy-like man is emerging.

As grieving families of days long gone came to these burial places, these paintings reminded them that what happened to Lazarus could happen to them. After all, the best stories in life—the ones that inspire us most—are about men and women who long for the same things we do. They are stories of people who encounter something or someone who changes the trajectory of their lives.

The story of Lazarus, an ordinary man living in the first century, is this kind of story. It inspired Italian Renaissance painters such as Giotto and Caravaggio to take brightly colored oils to plain white canvas and show us what mere words fail to convey. The Dutch painter Vincent van Gogh so identified with the story of Lazarus in his final years that he painted his own face as the transformed face of Lazarus emerging from the tomb. I'm currently in a season of feeling much the same way as van Gogh might have felt: Life is finally beginning to happen. I don't want to go back to the way it was. I want to live the life Jesus wants me to live. Do you?

If we hear of Lazarus today, it's usually standing at a freshly dug graveside. The pastor reads the famous words of Jesus: "I am the resurrection and the life. He who believes in me will live, even though he dies" (John 11:25). These words are supposed to bring comfort. But Jesus' words were *never* meant for the dead. They were meant for those who are alive—*we* are the people who need the message of Lazarus to bring hope to our weary lives. We are the ones who need transformation. *The Lazarus Life* offers us an opportunity to experience what we long for most.

Early in the book of John, we read about Jesus turning water into wine at a wedding celebration. He transforms water. Later, John shows

Jesus multiplying the loaves and fish to feed the thousands. He transforms loaves and fish. These miracles drew people to God. But when we come to John 11, we leave water and fish and loaves behind, and transformation takes place in flesh and blood—the life of an ordinary person named Lazarus. This one life so stirs us now that we wish it could be us.

MORE TO LIFE

Like Lazarus, you and I know what it is like to *not* be transformed.

- Unaffected by the power of God.
- Unaltered by the promises of Jesus.
- Impervious as a granite slab to the penetrating work of the Spirit.

It is possible to lead a wholesome life—one in which we maintain a job, marry a person we love, have children, bury our parents, and attend the church of our choice—and still miss out on what Jesus promised we could have. We might call it living a wholesome life of quiet desperation.

The spiritual life is first of all a *life* or it is no life at all. It is more than the emotions of love, hatred, passion, and desire, more than rationally deciding what to eat and where to sleep and what to believe. Yes, we are created by God to live a physical life with eyes that see, hearts that beat, and hands that touch. And yes, we are created to live an emotional life with passions and desires, and an intellectual life with our own will.

But many of the men and women I know and work with say they feel more dead than alive, more asleep than awake, more numb than passionate. Why is this so? Why do so many of us follow the teachings of Jesus and quietly ask, "Is this it? Is this the life Jesus told us about? Isn't there something *more*?" Lazarus shows us the "more" of life that you and I are thirsty for. More than what we know now—so that we can live before we die.

John the Baptist said it this way: "It's your life that must change, not your skin.... What counts is your life. Is it green and blossoming?" (Luke 3:8–9 MSG). The life Jesus describes in the story of Lazarus is not an improvement to our standard of living. It is not a secret to be learned or a formula to follow.[2] The spiritual life offered by Jesus, taught to us by Paul, and experienced by the early church, is a life of transformation. It is deep-down change at the DNA level of our souls. It is a life that comes only from Jesus, who identifies *Himself* as the only life we need.

SOUL-SICKNESS

It doesn't take us long in life to realize that what the Bible says is true: No one is sinless.[3] No one escapes being soul-sick. Our sickness seems to repeat itself across the pages and chapters of our lives. It even follows a predictable pattern: We make resolutions and promises to God, and we try to change, but we relapse. We take two steps forward but the one step back nearly always does us in. We muster up the energy to try to break an addiction, to rid ourselves of a self-destructive habit, to not be "so angry, so overweight, so anxious, so doubting, so obsessive, so selfish" or whatever it is (is there ever only one thing?) that brings dis-ease to our souls and makes us desperate.

This is what Dallas Willard calls "sin management"—when we use our own effort to try to control sin rather than dealing with it once and for all. A little bit of cyber-sex isn't as bad as being an addict, is it? A little bit of guilt, a little bit of anger, a little bit of envy is better than a life consumed with it, right? We try to manage our heart, mind, soul, and strength the best we can. All the while, however, the life that Jesus promised seems just beyond our grasp. The joy and passion that God intended for our lives feels like the cookie jar we'll never be tall enough to reach.

Aren't we tired of changing just enough to get by? Change from the outside might look good at church on Sunday, but it leaves us empty and restless the other six days of the week.[4] Pseudo-transformation doesn't touch our deepest soul-sickness. It doesn't move us beyond the issues, problems, and sins that keep us from experiencing the life Jesus promised.[5] Pseudo-transformation leaves us sick because when we don't really change, we have to live with the residue of guilt and shame over our repeated attempts to get life right.

A life outside the tomb is what we want. Real life. Authentic life. The abundant life that Jesus promises. The story of Lazarus offers us an opportunity to explore how transformation really happens—sometimes in the places we least expect it.

THE CEREAL STARE

Once upon a time, there was a little boy who joined his father every morning for breakfast. He sat down at the table hoping and longing for a time of substance with this man called Dad. But instead of engaging conversation or rib-tickling jokes or even, "What's on tap for today?" he was always served the same dish: the "Cereal Stare."

The Cereal Stare. The look that would overtake the father's eyes as his mind wandered to another country—a place of work deadlines, problems with a colleague, a crisis that had claimed his mind and heart, possibly even unfulfilled hopes and dreams. The father sat in this stare while the young boy looked on, always an arm's length away but never invited to this distant land.

The father chewed his Corn Flakes and the boy chewed his. The closest they came to one another was carrying their empty bowls to the kitchen sink. The father then went to work to engage in ways he could not or did not at home. The white Pontiac drove away, leaving the boy in the dust, unable to see his true way.

I began this chapter by saying, "I am Lazarus." And I am. However, once upon a time, Lazarus was a little boy. And I was too. The Corn Flakes were real. As was the little boy. And the father. It's difficult to write these words, for my intent is not to place blame, but to witness. Many of the men of my father's generation were emotionally distant. They found it difficult to give what they had never received themselves. It was for my dad. I understand that.

My father was a good provider. We always had breakfast on the table. But man doesn't live by breakfast alone. Neither do little boys. And the boy with a hungry heart grew into a man who was soul-sick—me. I cannot recall ever hearing the words from my father that I most needed and longed for: "I love you, Steve." I had to assume it. I had to imagine, guess, or suppose that I was loved and worthy to be loved. Through the chapters of my life, this same theme—the need to hear I was loved, accepted, and validated—emerged and reared its head like a dragon. I would fight and wound the dragon momentarily, but the beast refused to die. My soul-sickness crept into every job I had, every friendship I developed, and every person I touched, even my wife and sons. I routinely found myself distant, captured in a stare of my own. Harry Chapin's 1974 hit "Cat's in the Cradle" became all too true for me: I had grown up to be just like Dad.

WHEN LOVE IS WITHHELD

Psychologists tell us that self-love is either acquired in life or it is non-existent. No one is born with it. As children we look to our mothers and fathers to give our hearts what they so desperately need. In these early years things can go wonderfully right, and this is also the season of our lives when things can go woundingly wrong.

When love is withheld, the heart cannot thrive. Life without love has no meaning apart from doing things, performing, producing, and achieving. When affirmation, acceptance, and self-worth are withheld from us, or not nurtured to grow within us, we're left with holes. And we've got to fill the holes with something. Far too early we learn grown-up words like:

Achieve.

Strive.

Acquire.

Conquer.

This is exactly what I did. I learned how to be loved by doing, per-forming, and achieving. I became a go-getter so that I would be going somewhere—anywhere that I could feel loved. I sold the most tickets to the school barbecue and was rewarded for doing so. I became funny so I would be liked. I was responsible so that I would be respected. I earned love from others, and I tried to earn love from God. I lived in the land of the if-then's:

If I was good, then …

If I was committed, then …

If I went to church multiple times a week, then …

The more I did these things, the more celebrated and valued I felt. People applauded when I quoted Scripture. Men shook my hand and women produced teary-eyed smiles when I told them at five years of age, "I'm going to be a missionary to China." In those tender years I, like so many people, learned to live out of two stories: One was public and the other was very private—reserved only for those I felt would understand me. Those private stories are where the work of transformation is so desperately needed.

In public I learned the system, and I worked it. To be loved, I needed to do the right things, act the right way, and accomplish great tasks. A young man or woman can do this quite well for several decades, which is exactly what I did. I did extraordinary things for approval and acceptance.

I put all my trophies, jobs, and accomplishments in those holes in my soul. But the ache would not quit. My heart knew that something was wrong. All of my achieving was not filling a heart that was needy for love—simple love. In close relationships, demanding work, and inner longings, my soul-sickness showed up again and again. I've been on a long road to discover that no man as a friend, woman as a lover, or vocation as significance can offer me what Jesus offered Lazarus—life.

The story of Lazarus invites us into the truth that transformation does not begin with earning love. Transformation does not depend on our efforts to "make" it happen. Transformation begins when you *are* loved. This is what happened to Lazarus. Earthly flesh and blood can never speak this kind of deep love to our hearts. Only the Voice of Love will do. Only love transforms. Not power. Not coercion. Not programs. Not tips and techniques. Only love—and only the love of God.

EVERY SOUL NEEDS HEALING

Your concerns and soul-sickness may not be the same as mine, but something is bringing your soul a dis-ease—a longing for something different from the life you've been living so far. What is your soul-sickness? The holes in your soul? What are you living with that you wish you could change about yourself?

The name *Lazarus* means "whom God helps." We need Jesus' help just as Lazarus did. When we find ourselves sick and tired of being sick and tired, only God's help will do. The same breath that filled the deflated lungs of Lazarus and brought him back to life can be breathed into you and me. The same sickness—the sickness of thinking we can earn God's love—that brings death has an answer in Jesus.

This tightly bound and mummified Lazarus emerges with the only thing that matters—the only thing that really counts. Life—sheer, unbridled, and resurrected life—is finally his. And because I believe we're all Lazarus, it can be ours, too.

JESUS DID MORE THAN MAKE A POINT

The Bible is full of stories like that of Lazarus, stories that go far beyond statements of fact. They confront us with a truth that engages the mind while seeping into the soul. Not simply truth—transforming truth. Truth that will unlock our hearts and prepare our minds to understand the mysteries of the spiritual life. Through story we can enter the drama of what is being told. Our senses are engaged; we can touch and hear and see and smell and taste all the things that facts are unable to deliver. Through Jesus' masterful use of metaphor, we become the prodigal son, the rocky soil, the shepherd searching for a lost sheep in danger.

A good story offers a window to peer through in order to see something we could never come up with on our own. A great story ignites something within us that can't be ignored and will never be forgotten. A good story informs us. A great story changes us.

So as you enter the story of Lazarus, put yourself in the Middle Eastern village of Bethany two thousand years ago. Feel the hot breeze on your face and the sun-baked dirt under your feet. Through your own God-given five senses, experience for yourself how one ordinary person can change.

To help you discover this incredible story with all your senses, the artist Giotto's rendering of the story of Lazarus is inside the front cover of this book.[6] It is one of my favorites. All the characters that John mentions are in this incredible scene that Giotto has magnificently captured. By reading the story of John and through Giotto's brush with oils, we can see ourselves as really being *in* the story. As we move into the story, we'll examine some of the different characters, and we'll look at how their reactions and insights to what happened that day might inform our own lives today. I'll refer to the painting from time to time and I hope you will as well. It is a powerful image with the ability to prompt thought, reflection, and prayer.

Lazarus's story is not a sermon illustration, it's not a humorous anecdote, and it's not a formula for feeling good about the life of faith. It's nothing less than a gritty, sometimes raw, and gloriously real-life demonstration of spiritual transformation. When we enter this story, we will experience not just good ideas about how we can be transformed by God. We will experience true transformation.

God is kind, but he's not soft.
In kindness he takes us firmly by the hand
and leads us into radical life-change.
(Rom. 2:4 MSG)

NOTES

[1] This is how Eugene Peterson translates Jesus' famous words in John 10:10 where we are told that Jesus came to give us "real and eternal life, more and better life that they (we—you and I) ever dreamed of." (MSG).

[2] Jesus said, "These words I speak to you are not mere additions to your life, homeowner improvements to your standard of living. They are foundation words, words to build a life on (Luke 6:47 MSG).

[3] Verses that help us understand our soul-sick status include: Romans 3:23, 6:23; 1 John 1:8–10.

⁴ Jesus' strong words about the fallacy of outside change were directed at the Pharisees who sought external changes but neglected lasting inside-out change. See Matthew 23:25–26.

⁵ A more thorough description of the contrasts between transformation and pseudo-transformation is found in *The Transformation of a Man's Heart* (Downers Grove, IL: IVP, 2006), Stephen W. Smith, editor.

⁶ Giotto di Bondone was an Italian pre-Renassiance painter whose work paved the new way for painters to express emotion and character in his art. Born in 1267, in Florence, Italy, Giotto's work allowed him to become well-known and widely praised both during his life until the present. For more information on Giotto de Bondone and other artists who painted Lazarus's resurrection, see www.lazaruslife.com.

Chapter Two

THE LINGERING JESUS:
WAITING FOR HIS PRESENCE

When he heard that Lazarus was sick,
he stayed where he was two more days.

—John 11:6

- One of the mysteries of the spiritual life is that sometimes Jesus doesn't come when we need him most.
- Waiting for Jesus to arrive is part of the transformation process.
- Transformation involves working through our disappointments and disillusionments in life.
- We have hope in our transformation when we realize that we see today, and God sees eternity.

I magine the scene: Mary and Martha realizing that their brother is so ill that he might not live. How wonderful that their dear friend Jesus is in the region! The two sisters send word to Jesus that His dear friend is sick. They assume Jesus will come. Hadn't He healed others He'd never even talked to before? But Jesus doesn't show up. He does not heed the pleas of the sisters who beg for Him to come. He stayed where He was.

It would be tempting to try and determine just where Jesus was in relation to his dying friend. There are dozens of theories about the location of "Bethany beyond the Jordan," the last known locale of Jesus before the Lazarus story begins (John 10:40–42). But if we trust the story, we find that the place is not necessarily of prime importance. Had it been, it seems that John would have stressed that fact. What *is* emphasized is that Jesus heard the news and decided to stay longer, where he was (wherever that was) for two more days. The important matter is not so much the "where" as it is the "what." And the "what" is that Jesus lingered.

Where is God? Why doesn't He do something? Questions such as these must have been swirling in the hearts of Jesus' three friends from Bethany. Jesus, their friend, the One they believed in, didn't show up in their moment of greatest need. It must have seemed that He was not only "beyond" their physical surroundings, but also "beyond" caring about His dying friend. *Can't God see we need Him? Doesn't He care?*

When I enter the story of Lazarus and realize that Jesus did not immediately arise and go to Bethany, I have to admit I'm bothered. I'm bothered because a rapid response seems like the Christlike thing to do when someone is in need. But Jesus didn't drop what He was doing and ride to the rescue. He left the worsening Lazarus, the anxious Martha, and the worried Mary to themselves and to the reality of death. He lingered. Jesus stayed right where He was for two more days (v. 6).

Why did He stay away for so long when He was needed so desperately? Needed so desperately, in fact, that because of His absence, Lazarus died. The hearts of those who waited and waited and waited for Jesus to show up must have been chaotic with questions, anger, and confusion. When Jesus doesn't show up today, we struggle to navigate that same chaos in our own hearts. Does He not care for us?

WHY DOES JESUS LINGER?

Mary and Martha seemed smug in the way they approached the situation. After all, they knew Jesus was a busy man. He had lots of people to see and many things to do. Even so, they told Him, "Lord, the one you love is sick" (v. 3), reminding Him of His love for Lazarus, hoping this would persuade Him to leave all the other regular sick people and heal their brother. Yet for two full days, forty-eight hours, Jesus went on doing whatever Jesus did that is not recorded by the eyewitnesses of His life.

The sisters might have been expecting Jesus to do what He did for the centurion who simply asked Jesus to "say the word"—even from a distance—and the ill servant would be healed (Matt. 8:5–13). Mary and Martha might have said: "Jesus, You love Lazarus! Everyone knows You do. So just heal him from where You are and all people will praise You and know that You are the Messiah." Healing Lazarus from a distance would have been glorious, don't you think? But that didn't happen; in fact Jesus didn't even send a word that He'd be there ASAP! He lingered. Do you know this word—*linger*?

Mary and Martha might have felt entitled to Jesus' presence, think-ing that Jesus *should* do something for them because after all, they so often cared for Him. Surely He would now help them in their moment of need.

When Jesus didn't answer the pleas of Mary and Martha, they prob-ably realized they didn't know Him as well as they thought they did. Because as the hours of waiting turned into days, Jesus did not meet their expectations. And He may not meet ours. In the story of Lazarus, Jesus redefines *normal* for all of us. The lingering Jesus does not offer a guarantee that things will work out as we think they should.

When Jesus heard about Lazarus's condition, did He withdraw "to lonely places" to pray as Luke says He did at times (Luke 5:16)? Did solitude and silence assuage His grieving heart over Lazarus's gloomy illness? When I get upset, I want to eat and eat everything in sight. When my wife is anxious, she busies herself with cleaning the house and weeding the flower garden. When my best friend is concerned about something or someone, he goes on long bike rides in the moun-tains to "work it out." Whatever Jesus was doing, it must have seemed unimportant to Mary and Martha as they waited for Him to arrive.

Maybe Jesus did want to hightail it back to Bethany, but this was one of those moments when He had to submit His own will to that of the Father's. We have some evidence that Jesus was in the wilderness region where Satan tempted Him for forty days. Possibly this moment held the same kind of weight for Jesus: *If You are the Son of God, rush back and save Your friend.* Maybe Jesus was ready to go help His dying friend but the Father told Him, "No, My Son, You can't do what You want to do here. A greater plan is at work. It's not time yet."

Mary and Martha were left in the spiritual quandary of *if only*. *If only* Jesus had come. *If only* they had been more persuasive in their wording of the message intended for Jesus. *If only* Jesus really understood. *If only* He knew how sick Lazarus really was.

When we feel alone in our own circumstances or soul-sickness, our minds race with similar questions. Why do our prayers remain unanswered? Do our problems even concern a cosmos-pervading God? The last thing Jesus told His disciples before ascending into heaven was, "I am with you always, to the very end of the age" (Matt. 28:20). So where is He when we need him to help us the most? The God who lingers. The Jesus who makes other plans. The Spirit who hovers but never comes down to where we are. Isn't He Emmanuel— God with us?

Did Jesus ascend the steps of the World Trade Center while it was imploding, or was He lingering somewhere else? Does Jesus go to Darfur or is He lingering in a quieter place? Does He linger outside of surgical suites while doctors struggle to save a life? Does He linger from the woman who never married and always wanted to be? Does He linger when a child is being abused and no one is there to protect her?

I have to admit it yet again—these things bother me. They're but a new twist on the age-old question: Why does a loving God allow so much suffering in the world?

LIVING IN-BETWEEN

As we read the story of Lazarus, we have the advantage of knowing that Jesus *did* show up—eventually. But Mary, Martha, and the dying

Lazarus only knew that God was absent. For days of silence, they only knew the tomb.

Just like Mary and Martha, we live in an in-between time in many areas of our lives. In the midst of illness, doubt, and weakness, we try to keep hope in our hearts that when Jesus finally shows up, everything will be all right—but how will we make it through the waiting? "Living by faith is a bewildering venture. We rarely know what's coming next, and not many things turn out the way we anticipate. It is natural to assume that since I am God's chosen and beloved I will get favorable treatment from God who favors me so extravagantly."[1]

This in-between time—this "bewildering venture"—is a necessary experience in the spiritual life. It cannot be skipped or shortened, though many of us try to do exactly that. The invitation is to trust a God who makes us wait. Our fear is that Jesus may not show up for us—not now, perhaps not ever. In this in-between time, seismic earthquakes of doubt can topple our belief systems.

Many of us trade our confidence in God and faith in Jesus for what has been called "functional atheism."[2] Functional atheism says life is up to us and no one else. We have to do something—anything—to fix our daily crises and spiritual dilemmas. God isn't around; perhaps God doesn't even exist. Author Parker Palmer writes that functional atheism is at work when we say "pious words about God's presence in our lives but believe, on the contrary, that nothing good is going to happen unless we make it happen."[3]

Living in the in-between times can make even the most devout person succumb to these "pious words." Rather than wait for God, we work to bring about our own transformation. Yet the story of Lazarus indicates that in this awkward season, when it seems we are on our own, God is at work. Unseen. Unnoticed. Seemingly uninvolved. Quietly He is "God with us." The psychiatrist Gerald May founded the Shalom Institute for Spiritual Formation. In the last book he wrote before his death to cancer, he describes how the in-between times, when God seems absent, are precisely when God is at work. May uses nature and the season of winter's apparent dormant power to help us comprehend this important spiritual season. He writes:

> Deer and rabbits quiet, fish and frogs and turtles nearly
> frozen, snakes holed up, summer birds gone away and win-
> ter birds now here, trees black and bare, seeds and cocoons
> and grubs and cicada larvae and everything underground,
> deep inside, down and in where you cannot see the life
> happening. Life is rich in the time of keeping still, sap
> flowing, cells curing, change taking place.... Inside us all,
> in depths of our winters, things are going on, things we
> will have no clue of until spring comes, and perhaps, not
> even then.[4]

Experiencing the Jesus who lingers means having no clue as to what is happening in you or around you. In the full wake of winter's fury, you don't even know if spring will come. The winter is all you know. It's all that is real. The rest may be nothing more than a dream.

Today, I am in between the life I want to live and the life I am living. I am in between the faith I want to have and the doubts that rise up within me. I am in between becoming the person God wants me to be and the person I am right now. I am in between heaven, where it will all be worked out, and earth, where I have to live now.

We are like Mary, Martha, and Lazarus in so many ways. We cling to the belief that new life will come, but in the meantime we struggle to believe anything is happening. In this waiting—in the in-between time—something deep happens to us. Something happens *within* us. That's the way it has to be, because if transformation is anything at all, it is change from the inside out, not the outside in. Outside-in change is cosmetic. It's the kind of temporary fix we are used to.

Lazarus teaches us that authentic transformation is possible, not only for himself but for us—the ones who need it now! That's the kind of change John the Baptist spoke about when he said, "It's your life that must change, not your skin" (Luke 3:8 MSG). The New Testament wildman goes on to tell us that God's Spirit will come "within"—"changing you from the inside out" (Luke 3:16 MSG).

The apostle Paul tells us, "I consider that our present sufferings are not worth comparing with the glory that will be revealed in us" (Rom. 8:18). In the moment, we don't see this glory; it's something that "will be." Right now we only see our predicament. The dilemmas we face consume us—being fired, being abused, being treated unjustly, being lonely, being sick, being a modern-day Mary or Martha or Lazarus. But something else is at work. Someone else is working in the in-between times.

WAITING TO BE TRANSFORMED

Waiting on Jesus is not a passive act. Waiting on Jesus is soul work. Author Henri Nouwen writes:

> The secret of waiting is the faith that the seed has been
> planted, that something has begun. Active waiting
> means to be present fully to the moment, in the convic-
> tion that something is happening where you are and
> that you want to be present to it. A waiting person is
> someone who is present to the moment, who believes
> that this moment is the moment.[5]

As we wait, we relinquish control, surrender our wills, give up our
false hopes, and realize that if anything is going to happen at all, it will
have to be God's doing.

Jeremiah reminds us, "When life is heavy and hard to take, go off
by yourself. Enter the silence. Bow in prayer. Don't ask questions: Wait
for hope to appear. Don't run from trouble. Take it full-face. The 'worst'
is never the worst" (Lam. 3:28–30 MSG). The silence of waiting seems
futile. Yet, as we will see, something happens while we wait that cannot
happen at any other time.

Through waiting we become more aware of God and ourselves.
As we grow in God-awareness and self-awareness, we sense something
happening to us. This is the slow work of transformation that cannot be sped up by Jesus showing up any earlier than what has been
orchestrated. Through waiting we become more curious about our souls
within and the world without. We wonder. Waiting is an invitation to
wonder, to think more deeply, to ponder, to contemplate—a lost art in
our mad-paced world. When we find ourselves in a modern-day Garden
of Gethsemane, such as a hospital waiting room, or an empty house
after divorce, or another day looking for work, waiting helps us define

what we want and what we need. We realize that our transformation is not up to us—it never was![6] If anything is to happen, God must do it. Through waiting our transformation is accomplished because God does what we cannot.

JESUS IS NEVER IN A HURRY

As Mary and Martha sat with Lazarus, as friends and relatives came weeping for their loss, as days passed after Lazarus was put in the tomb, I wonder if they thought about what they *did* know about their friend Jesus. How might His absence make sense in light of who He was? Because even when we don't have answers, we can hold on to the things we know to be true.

One truth that Mary and Martha already knew about Jesus is that He didn't hurry. In fact thirty years pass between Jesus' miraculous birth and the beginning of His public ministry. Matthew, Mark, and Luke, the biographers of Jesus' life, only tell us of one occasion from Jesus' childhood. The rest of His life is hidden. They have nothing to report of His transformational ministry, diverse activities, or miraculous works. We do not hear Him say, "I need to be about my Father's business," from age twelve until age thirty. He remained obscured from the needy world and hungry people for three decades—thirty years!

We might consider that and think, *What a waste of time!* In this waiting period social conditions were worsening under Roman authority. The political situation deteriorated under Herod's rule. The life expectancy in the first century was not more than the early forties due to illnesses and primitive conditions. During all this time

Jesus lingered in a carpenter's shop making footstools and benches. Showing us how to live would come later—when God saw fit and not before. Jesus appeared at the right time—"the fullness of time," from a heavenly perspective and that's all we know.

Jesus still has a way of appearing at a time that is not based on human calendars or digital clocks. The word *time* in Scripture has two meanings in Greek. *Chronos* is literal time that can be plotted. This is where we get the word *chronology*. Chronos refers to events happening in succession in periods of the past, present, and future. The other word for *time* that the New Testament writers use is *kairos*. Kairos time is far different than chronos time; it is "the appointed time in the purpose of God," a moment of undetermined length when Godlike activity interrupts the cosmos. It is a "time in between" sequential time when God breaks through.

On that hot day in Bethany when Lazarus died, no plea from the begging sisters or concerned disciples could move Jesus to operate in their human chronos timetable. Everyone had to wait for the kairos moment. Until that moment, Jesus would linger, Lazarus would grow weaker and die, and the grieving sisters would wail for their loss.

Like Mary and Martha, we have in mind the chronos time when Jesus should arrive. Our fast-moving world shapes not only our culture, but also our beliefs about how God *should* work. We find it hard to understand that transformation is a slow process.

Consider the potter forming clay on a whirling wheel. When a marring or blemish appears, he reworks the clay. He shapes the clay until it is transformed into the desired image. This is not a fast process; it is not meant to be. It is intentional, deliberate, and purposeful. It may look slow to the observer, but the potter has had the timing in mind all along. The potter, like Jesus, knows about kairos. In the end we see beautiful workmanship because the potter waited for just the right time.

A GREATER GLORY

L. B. Cowman was a missionary to China and married to a very sick man. When her husband became too sick to work, the couple returned to the United States where she cared for him for six more years before he died.

In her classic book, *Streams in the Desert*, Cowman writes about what she learned from the lingering Jesus during her husband's illness and death. One of her most powerful illustrations describes how she kept a bottle-shaped cocoon of an emperor moth for almost a year. She wondered how the mature insect would emerge from the tiny opening, but she didn't know that the pressure of such an emergence forced fluid into the wings. She writes:

> I happened to witness the first efforts of my imprisoned moth to escape from its long confinement. All morning I watched it patiently trying and struggling to be free. It never seemed able to get beyond a certain point, and at last my patience was exhausted. The confining fibers were probably drier and less elastic than if the cocoon had been left all winter in its native habitat, as nature is meant to be. In any case, I thought I was wiser and more compassionate than its Maker, so I resolved

to give it a helping hand. With the point of my scissors, I snipped the confining threads to make the exit just a little easier. Immediately and with perfect ease, my moth crawled out, dragging a huge swollen body and little shriveled wings! I watched in vain to see the marvelous process of expansion in which these wings would silently and swiftly develop before my eyes. As I examined the delicately beautiful spots and markings of various colors that were all there in miniature, I longed to see them assume their ultimate size. I looked for my moth, the loveliest of its kind, to appear in all its perfect beauty. But I looked in vain. My misplaced tenderness had proved to be its ruin. The moth suffered an aborted life, crawling painfully through its brief existence instead of flying through the air on rainbow wings.[7]

Transformation is slow, not because God does not love us, but because God has greater purposes in mind. Has it occurred to you that God wants you to be transformed even more than you do? Cowman goes on to write, "O shortsighted person that I am! How do I know that one of these pains or groans should be relieved? The farsighted, perfect love that seeks the perfection of its object does not weakly shrink away from present, momentary suffering.... With this glorious purpose in sight, He does not relieve our crying."[8]

While Mary and Martha were agonizing because of Jesus' absence, Jesus told his disciples that Lazarus's illness was "for God's glory so that

God's son may be glorified through it" (John 11:4). Mary and Martha were tied into an earthly view of death. Jesus knew that greater good would come. Jesus might have thought, *Maybe in My lingering they will come to want God's glory more than they want Lazarus to live. Perhaps My lingering will change the posture of their hearts to say, "Not my will but Your will be done."* This is only conjecture, but it touches on a mystery in the spiritual life that surpasses our own reasoning. When Jesus lingers, we have much to consider.

Glory talk goes beyond our horizontal perspective and allows the transcendent God to break through at the most unusual times. Glory talk is when God does something big and gets the credit, which is a hard thing to understand when we're in a crisis and just need God to show up. But seasons when God seems distant and quiet become the fodder for the fire in which glory begins to burn brightly.

The language of glory is the language of mystery. What might the disciples have thought about glory in their hand-to-mouth, dusty, earthly existence? But Jesus was ready to meet the needs of His friends with the mysteries of God.

THE POWER OF EXPECTATIONS

Some friends of ours recently bought a beautiful new home that they said was the "house of our dreams." They saw themselves entertaining on their beautiful deck watching Colorado sunsets over Pikes Peak. But after moving in, they quickly became annoyed by traffic from the busy interstate and by the train that blows its whistle several times a day nearby. Their "house of dreams" quickly revealed itself to be an illusion.

Their expectations were dashed. The home of their dreams caused them to face several illusions that needed to be "dis-illusioned."

As my friend Tim likes to remind me, "Disappointment is a result of unmet expectations." This is true for every aspect of our lives. What do I expect from my friends? From my spouse? From my career? From my kids? If I'm disappointed, did I expect the wrong things? How can I live in reality yet keep moving toward what I really want in life, church, and friendship?

Just as Lazarus's ordinary family members in Bethany had to deal with their disappointments with God, each other, and themselves, we have to deal with ours. Unmet expectations can create tremendous upheaval in the spiritual life. The Jesus who lingers gives us the opportunity to face our fantasies and illusions and embrace something greater.

DEALING WITH DISILLUSIONMENT

Whether we are conscious of it or not, many of us live with the illusion that "life should be easy" or "once you become a Christian, life falls into place." These two statements are more than statements. They reveal a heart that has fostered a false sense of reality. This unreality always leads to disappointment upon disappointment. We build a false foundation for the Christian life and our relationships.

The word *disillusionment* is normally used in a negative context as in being disappointed and in despair about something. But disillusionment has the potential of being a positive experience. *Disillusionment* means to be "stripped of false impressions or misconceptions." To be disillusioned means to give up false pretenses about God, ourselves, and others.

The British preacher Oswald Chambers, and more recently, author Gail MacDonald, have suggested that we should practice the "discipline of dis-illusionment."[9] This discipline leads us to identify and change the illusions we hold in our hearts about how life should work and how God should behave.

Chambers explains it this way:

> The refusal to be disillusioned is the cause of much of the suffering in human life. It works in this way—if we love a human being and do not love God, we demand of him every perfection and every rectitude, and when we do not get it we become cruel and vindictive; we are demanding of a human being that which he or she cannot give. There is only one Being Who can satisfy the last aching abyss of the human heart, and that is the Lord Jesus Christ.[10]

Chambers says what every pilgrim who struggles with the lingering Jesus needs to realize: Only Jesus Christ can satisfy the last aching abyss of our heart.

This realization gave me a "Lazarus moment"—a moment of insight, self-awareness, and God-awareness—in my own journey. In my soul-sickness I had wanted my own father to do for me what only Jesus can do—to love me unconditionally. I may not find complete healing from my childhood wounds in this life, but the truth of God's love was my beginning of breaking free from the grip that held my heart hostage regarding my earthly father and my heavenly Father.

Working through my illusions was the key. Accepting the truth of God's love set me free.

If Jesus is the only One Who can satisfy us, what do we do when even Jesus fails to show up? I can imagine Mary and Martha preparing Lazarus's body for burial, venting angry tears. Each tear rolled out more disappointment. Each groan revealed their disappointment in Jesus. They each lamented the same confession of disappointment to Jesus, "Lord, if you had been here, my brother would not have died!" (Martha in John 11:21 and Mary in John 11:32). Their shared confession reveals their shared illusion: Bad things will not happen if Jesus is present.

This illusion was the root of their devastating disappointment. Just like Mary and Martha, our illusions are the root of our devastating disappointments with God, one another and ourselves. Here's the truth: Illusions are what lead to disappointment and unfulfilled expectations.

A necessary part of the journey toward being a transformed person is practicing the discipline of disillusionment. We tend to hold on to so many illusions in our lives instead of embracing what is true. For example, illusions about what that "perfect" Christmas will be like, how that fairytale wedding will go, finally getting the job that weds a calling with the world's need, discovering that relationship that will fill the vacuum-shaped hole in the heart; these and more can fuel our disappointments in life and with each other. Facing our illusions offers us the opportunity to dis-illusion a false reality and to discover life-giving truth.

Jesus comforted the sisters with the truth, and the truth set the sisters free from their illusions. The truth is that Jesus redefined life as they knew it and as we know it today. Illusions breed false hope and a false life. Embracing the truth offers us freedom and true life. Here lies the invitation for each of us to live the Lazarus life: Embracing what is true is core of the transformed life. The Jesus who lingers helps us work through our disillusionments and discover more of the character of God.

It's ironic that the times when God seems most absent can be the times when we get to know Him better. We read in Romans 5:5 that "hope does not disappoint us." As our desperate hearts cry out to the lingering Jesus, we wonder what kind of hope that could be. It's in those moments that God is birthing a new hope in us, a hope in who He is, not a hope in who we want Him to be. It is a lifelong journey to understand that *who God is* will not disappoint us. Glory is brooding. Glory is about to be unleashed.

NOTES

[1] Eugene Peterson in the "Introduction to Habakkuk," *The Message/Remix* (Colorado Springs, CO: NavPress, 2006), 1378.

[2] Coined by Parker Palmer in *Let Your Life Speak*: Parker J. Palmer, *Let Your Life Speak* (San Francisco: Jossey-Bass, 2000), 64.

[3] Palmer, *Let Your Life Speak*, 64.

[4] Gerald G. May, *The Wisdom of Wilderness* (San Franciso: HarperSanFrancisco, 2006), 90.

[5] Henri Nouwen, "A Spirituality of Waiting: Being Alert to God's Presence in Our Lives," *Weavings,* January 1987 http://www.upperroom.org/weavings/

6 Sara Grove's song, "Remember, Surrender" is a song written from a tomb and
   offers insight about the concept of surrendering.

7 L. B. Cowman, *Streams in the Desert* (Grand Rapids, MI: Zondervan 1997),
   24–25.

8 Cowman, *Streams in the Desert*, 24–25.

9 Oswald Chambers introduced me to this idea in his wonderful "My Utmost
   for His Highest" devotional entry for July 30. Gail MacDonald elaborates on
   this in her book, *A Step Farther and Higher* (Multnomah, 1993).

10 Oswald Chambers, *My Utmost for His Highest* (Toronto: McClelland and
   Stewart Limited by Dodd, Mead & Company Inc., 1935), 212.

Chapter Three

TRAPPED IN THE TOMB:
WHEN LIFE COMES TO A DEAD END

*On his arrival, Jesus found that Lazarus
had already been in the tomb for four days.*
—John 11:17

- The tombs of our lives—the dark places of failure and pain—
  are where transformation begins.
- People often fail to recognize the reality of tombs.
- Entering our own tombs helps us face our need for God.
- God uses the tombs of our lives to reveal His true identity.

The lingering Jesus didn't just cut it close. He didn't make it. In the days that Mary and Martha waited for Jesus, Lazarus died. The unthinkable possibility had become reality. Lazarus entered a literal tomb of darkness and decay as Mary and Martha entered an emotional and spiritual tomb of longing, disappointment, and defeat. The tomb, not their embrace, would hold their brother.

Just as we often do in the spiritual life, Lazarus and his sisters had hit a dead end. Everything they'd believed about God was in question. There was no way out—or so they thought.

In the dark tombs of our lives, doubt can overtake hope in every moment. A divorce, a doctor's diagnosis, a church split, a job loss, or the death of a family member can bring us to a sudden darkness that seems impossible to escape. Or we might not be facing new circumstances at all—and that in itself leads us to a stagnant despair. Everything in life might appear to be going well, and yet our hearts our hemorrhaging from a past shame or a doubt so powerful that all we once believed about God suddenly seems uncertain. Whatever leads us to an emotional and spiritual tomb, we face a dark tomb indeed when God doesn't show up when we are expecting Him.

The tombs of our lives look much different when we're twenty than they do when we're fifty or seventy. Each decade of the journey seems to yield a different perspective on what really matters and what life is really about. Yet tomb-work is the same in each stage of life. We can run from our tombs or hide from them, but in the end, they are a necessary place for transformation to do its work because in the tombs of life we come to know God in a life-giving way.

THINGS AS THEY ARE

In the play *Les Miserables* by Victor Hugo, the prostitute Fantine lived in a tomb of dashed dreams and a pit of disillusionment. She had nourished a dream of a better life—as we all do in some way—yet the cruelty of those in power over her, the despair of poverty and tuberculosis, and the brutality of the French Revolution took away her hope and killed the dream for her life. In the Broadway musical Fantine sings of the dream she used to have in days gone by, the dream full of hope and life, the dream so different from what she finds herself living. She seems to sing for all of us:

> I dreamed a dream in time gone by ...
> I had a dream my life would be
> So different from this hell I'm living
> So different now from what it seemed
> Now life has killed the dream I dreamed.[1]

I've played Fantine's song in retreats and church settings as well as in private counseling sessions. The reaction is almost always the same. Stunned silence. How readily we identify with Fantine's plight and her wounded heart! This wayward woman speaks to our shattered dreams—men who were fired from jobs or who failed at relationships, women who can never achieve the air-brushed looks of magazine covers, injured athletes who can no longer compete on the sports field, a couple who lost a life's savings in a dot-com crash.

Fantine's words aggravate the scab in so many of us who are trying to recover from life's losses—to claw our way out of the tomb. The initial joy of becoming a Christian can fade on the long, arduous journey home. We feel trapped in a tomb that makes the life we once dreamed seem like a fantasy.

The famous missionary Amy Carmichael knew about literal and metaphorical tombs of life. Born in Ireland, Carmichael moved to India in 1895 and spent her life caring for the physical and spiritual needs of the people of the country, including thousands of orphaned children. For fifty-three years Amy Carmichael worked among the world's poorest people group, having never returned home to her native Ireland for a furlough.

Carmichael authored many books that still inspire Christians today. One of the books she wrote, however, was only reluctantly published by her mission-sending agency. It was titled, *Things as They Are*. In this true account of one season of her life, Carmichael shared the harsh realities of life in southern India. Her mission organization feared that a book describing the horrible conditions of her work would not be good promotional material for the mission and would not inspire young missionaries to take up the work. The organization asked Carmichael to write more encouraging stories with positive impact. But she stood courageously to tell the story just as it was with no embellishing or sugarcoating.

Perhaps we all have a book in our hearts like Amy Carmichael had—a book that speaks the truth so bluntly, so truthfully, so courageously, that it unsettles those around us who want to avoid facing the dark places of life. What happens to our soul's diaries, journals, and memoirs—our stories of unfulfilled longings and dashed desires? Are we not to speak of the realities of the spiritual life?

The tomb of Lazarus provides a powerful image of "things as they are" in the Christian life. My unpublished book of things as they are would include chapters on being fired; being betrayed by a close friend;

my wife being diagnosed with breast cancer and my panic at the thought of raising our four boys alone; my youngest son nearly dying in the Grand Canyon on a family outing; an author-friend dying at my feet in a rock climbing accident on a men's retreat ... I could go on.

We all have stories of dark tombs in our lives, times when the lingering Jesus simply did not show up, and we were left with no hope for the future. The thud of the rock being rolled against our own tomb becomes a dark reality.

THE PLACE OF RESURRECTION

After the much-loved friend of Jesus breathed his last breath of air, his body was prepared for burial. A quick burial was customary in those days because of the heat and environmental factors. The body was not embalmed; it was simply cleaned and then wrapped in strips of clothes. Spices were poured into the folds of the graveclothes to mask the smell of decay.

At this point in Lazarus's story, the grave was not "swallowed up in victory" (1 Cor. 15:54). His tomb, in fact, represents a place of theological crisis. Mary and Martha lost more than their brother in death. They lost their belief that life would be all right because they had Jesus figured out.

Just when we think we know God, something happens that erodes our nicely acquired theological foundations and formulas of faith. Wars in Iraq, tsunamis in Indonesia, and terrorist attacks in New York, Spain, and England jolt our faith. Individual loss shakes us as we face the daily pain of a parent's death or a child's illness, a stale marriage, the memory of sexual abuse, or a lifelong struggle with a hidden addiction. Questions rise up within us and around us: *What is happening? Where is God?*

Transformation is often sabotaged at this point because we don't allow suffering to do what only suffering can do: transform us. To fully appreciate the good news of Jesus, we must acknowledge the hard realities of our earthly life—in other words, the bad news. Yet in our efforts to lead spiritual lives, we rarely embrace the times when life feels like a tomb. We cushion the effects of pain by telling others we're "fine" and expecting them to say the same. We fill our lives with busyness, food, and hollow interactions just to avoid a quiet house at night.

A religion that does not embrace the tomb is only a feel-good religion, not an authentic relationship with God. If we fail to address the soul-stirring questions that the tombs of our lives ask, if we pretend that tombs do not exist, and we ignore the difficult parts of life and faith, then we will settle for something far less than authentic transformation. Our faith becomes sentimental. Our songs become folksy. Our prayers become hollow. Our sermons become talks. Our Bible becomes like any other book.

Without acknowledging the pain of life, we will not know the abundance of life that Jesus came to bring us. The tomb is where resurrection happens—in fact the tomb is the only place resurrection happens. The places in our hearts where failure reigns and despair rules are the places where transformation begins, not ends. We can have no life without first entering death.

PAUL'S TOMB

The apostle Paul was willing to recognize "things as they are" in the Christian life.

It's tempting to think that Paul had God all figured out—he often comes across in his writings that way. But Paul reveals his battered heart and despairing soul in 2 Corinthians 1:8–9:

> We do not want you to be uninformed, brothers, about the hardships we suffered in the province of Asia. We were under great pressure, far beyond our ability to endure, so that we despaired even of life. Indeed, in our hearts we felt the sentence of death.

What could have happened in Asia that left Paul feeling as if he could not endure it any longer, so deeply troubled that he despaired of life? Scholars are not sure as to what events Paul is referring. Was it a desperate illness like that of Lazarus? Was it another mob attack? Was it the betrayal of a friend?[2]

Whatever it was, it caused Paul to think the end of life was near. Consider how other translations help us see the reality Paul was in:

- "We were *crushed and overwhelmed* beyond our ability to endure, and we thought we would never live through it. In fact, we expected to die." (NLT)
- "For we do not want you to be *uninformed*, brethren, about the *affliction* and *oppressing distress* which befell us in [the province of] Asia, how we were *so utterly and unbearably weighed down and crushed* that we despaired even of life [itself]." (AB)
- "It was so bad we didn't think we were going to make it. We felt like we'd been sent to death row, that it was all over for us. (MSG)

Crushed, overwhelmed, affliction, oppressing distress, not going to make it, and *sent to death row.* These are the soul-jarring words of the writer of much of our New Testament. Paul knew something about dead ends, depression, and despair. He wasn't afraid to admit the way life was, and he didn't want to protect his readers from the staggering truth about it.

Paul felt no need to protect the reputation of God when he wrote these shocking words. He didn't feel the need to say, "Now I am going to tell you something that happened that was really bad but don't ever forget that God is good—all the time." Paul let the facts speak for themselves. He told it like it was. He described a reality of the spiritual life that we often fear putting words to.

Paul's words, like Lazarus's story, give us permission to acknowledge the times in our lives where it looks like the end. Finished. Over. We need the freedom to express our tomb-like thoughts instead of hiding behind spiritual clichés and Christianese—the language that does not speak of depression, despair, and disillusionment. Wouldn't more sermons, seminars, and books titled *Things as They Are* help us rather than hinder us in our relationship with God?

GOD ALONE

As Paul continues to share his dreadful experience, he writes that the hard things he described "happened that we might not rely on ourselves but on God, who raises the dead" (2 Cor. 1:9). The hard times stripped away false pretenses and softly held convictions in Paul's life.

This is precisely what the tomb times of our lives do—they strip us down so that no clothes can cover our vulnerability. Then we are naked before the God of resurrection power and true life. Every tomb gives God the opportunity to do the unthinkable. Every tomb becomes the sweet, dark place where God can do what only God can do.

Paul and Lazarus learned what we must learn. The beginning work of transformation does not begin with us. It begins with God. The cold, rigor mortis-filled body of Lazarus could do nothing but decay apart from God's transforming work. Without the work of transformation, our faith will become stiffened, our theology hardened, and our hearts congealed—unable to be moved, unable to sense God's presence, powerless to live the life Jesus intends for us to live.

The tomb reveals to us that apart from God we will not be changed. We are a part of our own transformation, as we will see, but ultimately it is not up to us to "self-help" our way out of the darkness. God is the one who delivers us. Paul says it this way, "He *has delivered* us from such a deadly peril, and *he will deliver* us. On him we have set our hope that *he will continue to deliver us*" (2 Cor. 1:9–10).

Paul knew of Lazarus. Paul knew that the God of the resurrection—the same God who got Lazarus up and alive, the same God who brought life back to Jesus—was capable of transforming any person or situation, no matter how dire the circumstances. Even tombs cannot prevent God's work of deliverance and transformation. When we realize we cannot free ourselves, that's when Jesus arrives.

NO TOMB DARK ENOUGH

God thrives in our lives when we find we have nothing else to hold onto. As L. B. Cowman writes, "Our almighty God is like a parent who delights in leading the tender children in His care to the very edge of a precipice and then shoving them off the cliff into nothing but air."[3] Jesus himself tells us, "You're blessed when you're at the end of your rope. With less of you there is more of God and his rule" (Matt. 5:3 MSG).

God has a soft place in His heart for ordinary people who find themselves desperate for change; in fact the Bible is full of them: the centurion's ill servant, the woman at the well, the man paralyzed for thirty-eight years at the pool of Siloam. Why haven't we learned to connect the dots to see where transformation happens most? Outside our own tombs of defeat and despair stands a crowd of ordinary men and women who faced their tombs and yet emerged as trophies of transformation.

Consider Joseph, who, while imprisoned in Egypt because of false accusations, underwent transformation and said of his brother's evil intentions, "You intended to harm me, but God intended it for good to accomplish what is now being done, the saving of many lives" (Gen. 50:20).

The prophet Daniel tried to do all the right things and honor God. Yet life backfired and Daniel found himself in the dead end of a lion's den. The king, worried about Daniel's ability to survive this ordeal, came early the next morning and exclaimed, "Daniel, servant of the living God, has your God, whom you serve continually been able to rescue you from the lions? … I issue a decree that in every part of my kingdom people must fear and reverence the God of Daniel" (Dan. 6:20, 26). Transformation began in a nation because of one man's dead-end circumstance.

The fearful prophet Jonah found himself in a place of transformation inside the belly of the whale. Peter was transformed through his denial of Jesus. Thomas was transformed through his mindful doubts. Paul was transformed despite his murderous rampage against Christians.

Here's the simple truth: God can use any circumstance, any tragedy, any wronged heart as an instrument for our transformation. No tomb is dark enough, no situation hard enough, no life broken enough that God cannot use it as fodder for the fire of transformation.

SPEAKING IN PARADOX

"It was the best of times, it was the worst of times, it was the age of wisdom, it was the age of foolishness, it was the epoch of belief, it was the epoch of incredulity, it was the season of light, it was the season of darkness, it was the spring of hope, it was the winter of despair."[4]

Spiritual transformation requires learning to speak in this kind of paradox. How is this reality possible? Surely it's either the best of times *or* the worst of times, not both at once. When Paul told us about "things as they are" in his life, he introduced us to speaking about our life in paradox. Yes, he spoke of trouble, but he also spoke of comfort in the same sentence. He said: "the Father of compassion and the God of all comfort who comforts us in all our troubles ..." (2 Cor. 1:3–4). We wonder how trouble and comfort can coexist. Surely it must be *either* comfort *or* trouble—not both at the same time. But this is now how Paul speaks and Paul gives us permission to speak in paradox as well.

Have you ever heard someone say, "It was the absolute worst time of my life, *but* God was closer to me than I've ever felt"? Or how about, "I didn't think I would survive my husband's death, *but* God gave me a peace I had never known before"?

Speaking in spiritual paradox allows us to be fluent in the entire language of the spiritual life. Remember, if we only speak of blessings and positive aspects of the Christian life, we are not embracing the whole truth. Life with Jesus *does* bring joy, hope, and a peace that we cannot find in any other relationship. Yet we first meet Jesus when we are tied to earth, and that means that earthly deaths, doubts, and sins still reach us. Before we can be resurrected, we must die. If we do not become fluent in the language of paradox, then we hide our needs, drown our desire to change, and ignore our soul's desperate longing to be transformed way down deep.

THE NEED FOR TRANSFORMATION

I went through a season in my life when I thought my wife and I were happily married, but I was wrong. We had four young sons and I was called to lead a large church in North Carolina as the senior pastor. It felt like heaven for me. A large staff. A suite of offices. My own assistant. I thought I had arrived.

Because of my own soul-sickness and need for affirmation, I poured my heart and soul into my work. Unaware of what I was really doing, I developed an addiction as nasty as heroin and as dark as meth. My addiction was my work, and the dark side of my own addiction was that I was applauded for working hard. The more praise I got, the more I worked. My church mushroomed, which only affirmed the toxicity of my addiction. Success often has a dark side and my dark side revealed its ugly belly in my marriage and home life. The truth was I really didn't have a home life. I had a work life and a place to change clothes and take a shower.

The tomb began to close in on me one day when my wife went to see her doctor. The doctor took time to ask Gwen questions about her life as the mother of four boys under age ten and the demands of being a pastor's wife. Then at some point during the physical examination, the doctor noticed a rash under her wedding ring. She asked Gwen, "Has this been there a long time?" Gwen sheepishly said, "Yes, a very long time." Then the doctor spoke words that would be a turning point in our marriage. "Gwen, when I see a rash like this, it makes me wonder if there is a rash in the marriage. Is there?"

When Gwen told me this, I barked out that the doctor was a quack. What did a rash on a finger have to do with the intimacy of our marriage? I dismissed this cry for help from my wife and her doctor as nonsense and went on with my life. Then just a few weeks later, the door of the tomb came crashing down.

It happened after Gary Chapman, author of the best-selling *The Five Love Languages,* came and led a marriage retreat at our church. He spoke on how we give and receive love through five primary *languages*: acts of service, gifts, words of affirmation, physical touch, and quality time. Gwen and I sat in the final service near the front of our palatial sanctuary listening to Gary teach us. My oldest son, Blake, sat with us. After the service we raced home to have Sunday dinner. I had to get back for a meeting with our leaders at 2:00 p.m. because of something pressing. This season of my life was always ruled by the "tyranny of the urgent." At lunch I asked my boys what they learned at church earlier that morning. I said to my oldest, "Blake, any idea what your love language is?" Blake stalled as if he was searching his heart for the answer—but he already knew the answer. Finally he said, "Dad, I know my love language. It is quality time, and I never get any from you."

The tomb was sealed. I was at the dead end. My firstborn son had exposed my heart and shattered my world. I had become a modern-day Abraham, willing to sacrifice my firstborn son, not because God told me to, but because the sacrifice of time with him seemed to get in the way of my life, my career, my addiction.

I had to face the reality of a wife diagnosed with a cancerous rash in our marriage and a son who felt rejected and unloved. I had become my father. The Cereal Stare had been replaced by the Church Stare. My sons were experiencing me in the same way I experienced my father. Could the cycle be broken? Desperate for change I went to a counselor for help, where I gained valuable insight about myself—something I was woefully ignorant of. (In chapter 8, we'll explore how others help us on the journey toward transformation.)

I then discovered these words from John Calvin's *Institutes*: "There is no deep knowing of God without a deep knowing of self and no deep knowing of self without a deep knowing of God."[5] This is why the tombs of our lives are such a spiritual asset. They help us to become more self-aware and more aware of our need for God. The tomb becomes a room of mirrors for us to see ourselves as we are.

I had been fooled in my theological journey and in my pursuits as a pastor to think that getting more information about God was all that mattered. In fact many of us in the West mistakenly believe that transformation happens when we get more information and get all the facts straight. Many of the programs developed for Christians today are based on this false assumption. More teaching, more seminars, and more notebooks do not result in a transformed life! If that were so, I'd be 100 percent transformed due to the size of my bookshelves and number of conferences I have attended. The tombs of life teach us that information alone does not lead to a transformed life. Neither does trying harder or wallowing in shame and blame because of all of our failed attempts.

My journey toward transformation required me to take a long look at my childhood and my personal soul-sickness and see how I had gotten to this dead-end place in life. Augustine, the famous theologian and writer, prayed something similar in his *Confessions:* "Grant Lord, that I may know myself that I may know thee." Spiritual transformation requires a gut-level honesty about our fears, disappointments, disillusionments, and failures.

My life changed because my son, my wife, and a physician spoke about "things as they are." Perhaps this is one meaning of the admonition to confess our sins to one another (James 5:16). If we don't speak of our tombs with each other—and admit the truth of our bankrupt longings and desires—we remain in the dark; the light of each other's presence and companionship in the tomb cannot be shared.

We are transformed when we allow God to do what information fails to do. We are transformed when we look at our lives and become aware of our real condition—no matter how bad it is—and face the truth about ourselves, God, the past, the present, and the future.

SOUL CARE

My transformational journey to reclaim my wife and become a transformed father required a stopover in a monastery in Southern California. I didn't consider myself the monastery type, but I was so sick and tired of being sick and tired that I was willing to try almost anything. I was told the monastery would teach me "the ways of Jesus." That intrigued me since my way was not working. *Perhaps*, I thought, *I still have something to learn.*

This monastery became a cocoon for me to enter. For one month I read the great Christian classics, took long walks alone, and experienced silence for the first time in my life. I met with author Dallas Willard, and throughout the days he allowed me to hemorrhage and heal, lament and languish, pray and ponder my life thus far.

My soul-sickness had compelled me to commit the sin of busyness—which, as Willard says, is the only sin that the church celebrates. Busyness assured me of my identity and somehow seemed to assuage my need to be loved. My busy work gave me the significance my soul craved so deeply. As an extrovert I was afraid of solitude. As a person who loves to talk, I was suspicious of silence. Yet in silence I began to find my true self and discover a heart embedded within me that had gotten lost along the way. In silence I began to listen to Jesus' personal invitation to receive his love.

I'd always thought that people who needed solitude were weak. At the monastery, however, I discovered the truth of Henri Nouwen's words: "Solitude is the furnace of transformation."[6] For the very first time in my life, I entered that place called solitude and my heart found the rest and healing that I had always been looking for.

Those weeks in that secluded monastery were like a detox program for me. The influence of that experience radically transformed my marriage, my relationships with my children, my philosophy of ministry, and my understanding of how a person really changes. Now Gwen and I have our own ministry called The Potter's Inn, which offers a prophetic voice calling to people like me to consider a better way to live. We offer Christ's heart of companionship for those who are in the tomb. We call it soul care. The Potter's Inn offers a 360-degree walk around a person's life, helping him or her explore his or her own soul-sickness and ways to experience transformation.

So, out of my own soul-sickness came a desire to help people with a similar diagnosis learn the ways of Jesus' life and teaching. As we will see in Lazarus's story, there is no end to the influence of a life in the process of transformation.

SWEET DARKNESS

M. Craig Barnes writes, "The transforming moment in Christian conversion comes when we realize that even God has left us. We then discover it was not God, but our image of God, that abandoned us. This frees us to discover more of the mystery of God than we knew. Only then is change possible."[7] God uses the dead-end times in life to reveal his true identity. The Jewish prophet Isaiah hints at this when we hear God speaking:

I will give you the treasures of darkness,
riches stored in secret places,
so that you may know that I am the LORD,
the God of Israel, who summons you by name.
(Isa. 45:3)

Without the darkness of the tomb, we will still walk in our own light and attempt to live what we think is life. Darkness reveals the richness of the life that only Jesus gives.

St. John of the Cross wrote about this beautiful, difficult paradox in his spiritual classic, *The Dark Night of the Soul*. Today people often speak of their "dark night of the soul" being a place of abandonment and utter aloneness, but this is not what St. John meant. For St. John the dark night was a sweet night, a night of true communion with the Divine. This is the paradox of the tomb. This is what so many spiritual writers have attempted to tell us. The end is never the end. The end is a beginning of understanding and real life.

Sometimes it takes darkness and the sweet
confinement of your aloneness
to learn
anything or anyone
That does not bring you alive
Is too small for you.[8]

You may be aware of something or someone that is not making you feel alive. You may be facing a dead end and sensing the thud of the stone sealing you in. But the sweet darkness can remind you of something else—of Someone else who is there with you. The truth is, you do not belong in the tomb. Every tomb of life is too small for you. It is the brief interlude before the abundant life you were meant to live, before the reality of transformation, before the moment you hear Jesus speaking into the darkness.

NOTES

[1] "I Dreamed a Dream," Herbert Kretzner, from *Les Miserables,* 1985

[2] To survey some of Paul's perils, see 2 Cor. 11:23–27, 1 Cor. 15:32, and Acts 19:23–41.

[3] Cowman, *Streams in the Desert,* 369.

[4] Charles Dickens, *Tale of Two Cities* (Pocket Books of Simon & Shuster Inc., 2004 edition), 5.

[5] John Calvin, *Institutes of the Christian Religion,* 1536 ed./trans. Ford Lewis Battles (Grand Rapids, MI: Eerdmans, 1995), 15.

[6] Henri Nouwen, *The Way of the Heart* (New York: Ballantine Books, 1981), 16.

[7] M. Craig Barnes, *When God Interrupts* (Downers Grove, IL: IVP, 1996), 123.

[8] David Whyte, "Sweet Darkness" in *The House of Belonging* (Langley, WA: Many Rivers Press, 1996), 23.

Chapter Four

THE VOICE OF LOVE:
HEARING YOUR SAVIOR CALL YOU BY NAME

Jesus called in a loud voice ...
—John 11:43

- In the story of Lazarus, we learn three of the most important words of the spiritual life.
- Our lives change when we realize that God loves us as individuals more than He loves the entire world.
- Only love transforms.

We know the end of the story: resurrection. Mary and Martha, standing outside their brother's tomb, knew only death. When Jesus did arrive and stepped toward the tomb, no one in the crowd knew what He would say. We can imagine how silent it might have been. In this awkward quiet, hearing the footsteps of Jesus move toward the tomb in determination must have been stunning. All eyes were riveted on Him. One could hear only muffled whispers of doubters and perhaps the prayers of His friends to do the unthinkable, the unprecedented, the amazing work ahead of Him.

So after the lingering, after the days of the tomb, Jesus moved step-by-step toward the man He deeply loved. Each step marked love's determination to transform Lazarus. Each step defined the radical power of love. Jesus stood at the entrance to the tomb and spoke the three most important words Lazarus would ever hear: "Lazarus, come forth."

The crowd standing by the tomb's entrance waited. Would anything happen? How could speaking his name bring him back to life? The quietness of that hot afternoon was suddenly stirred with movement from within the tomb. Life. Change. Transformation.

Love would not be impotent in the face of death's grip. Love would speak. Love would act. Love would transform. The Word now made flesh would speak something from the depths of His own soul that defied death's power and revealed the Father's glory. Nothing could match love's power. Nothing. When love speaks, we will awaken to its voice.

John goes further than any other New Testament writer to reveal to us that God's voice is not the voice of wrath, condemnation, hatred, or rejection. No matter what we have grown up believing about Jesus, the story of Lazarus shows us that Jesus speaks in the Voice of Love. This is a point where we need to be sure and dis-illusion ourselves.

In Jesus' words to Lazarus, we hear the same Voice of Love that we can hear for ourselves today. We learn through Lazarus that only love transforms a person—not power, information, or effort. We learn through Lazarus the beauty of *listening* to that love. This is one of the greatest spiritual callings of our journey.

Lazarus's body and soul were lifeless. Unresponsive. Rigor mortis had set in. Perhaps these words describe your spiritual life right now. Has your career come to a dead end? Is your marriage dancing on thin ice? Does God seem so far off that you can't imagine hearing Him speak to you?

Hearing Jesus speak your name is the first step in emerging from the tomb and moving toward transformation. Jesus speaks *your* name— not your friend's, not your pastor's, not your teacher's—when He invites you to "come forth." It is a personal invitation of love.

JESUS LOVES THE ORDINARY INDIVIDUAL

One of the most famous verses in the Bible is found just a few chapters before the story of Lazarus: "For God so loved the world that he gave his one and only Son, that whoever believes in him shall not perish but have eternal life" (John 3:16). This verse speaks of God's expansive love. The whole world is loved by God. Yet when John tells us the story of Lazarus, we do not hear that God loves the world. We hear that God loves *specific and ordinary people who live in the world*. Up until this point in John's gospel, no specific individual is named as the benefactor or recipient of God's love. But now everything changes. The beloved apostle narrows God's love from a huge, impersonal world to a specific individual: Lazarus. As John tells the story, we learn:

- "Lord, the one [Lazarus] you *love* is sick" (John 11:3).
- "Jesus *loved* Martha and her sister and Lazarus" (John 11:5).
- "Then the Jews said, 'See how he (Jesus) *loved* him (Lazarus)'" (John 11:36).

John goes so far as to say that Lazarus is Jesus' "friend" (11:11) even before the rest of the followers of Jesus are named "friends" (John 15:13–15). In Lazarus love gets specific. And when love gets specific, transformation happens.

Having four children, I can say, "I love all of my children." But this is not what each son needs and wants. Each of my sons wants to hear me say *his* name. He wants to know that he matters to me in a personal and specific way. In the same way, we long to know that God loves us as individuals. Human love can do this for a few but only Sacred Love can love each one of us. Loving en masse is something a benevolent dictator does for his people; loving with distinction is something only God can do.

Christian psychologist and author David Benner tells us, "There is nothing more important in life than learning to love and be loved.... Love speaks to the depths of our soul, where we yearn for release from isolation and long for the belonging that will assure us we are at last home."[1] The story of Lazarus becomes a defining moment in our own spiritual journey because it reminds us that we are the objects of *God's* love, just as Lazarus was. Learning to let yourself be loved is *the* crucial step toward being a transformed man or woman. Let me repeat: The crucial step in being transformed is learning to let yourself be loved. Skip this step and transformation will not happen.

MOVING FROM THE HEAD TO THE HEART

In the Western world most of us build our faith upon a system of beliefs about God. We form these beliefs into creeds and confessions of faith. We say them in our churches. Our pew racks hold them printed on reminder cards. But we need to *experience* God's *love* if we are to be transformed by it.

It has been said, "The longest, most arduous journey in the world is often the journey from head to heart. Until that roundtrip is complete, we remain at war within ourselves."[2] A journey must take place from the head to the heart if we are to be transformed at all. We must truly experience this love that God has for each one of us. Without that experience we will believe we are living, but we'll be void inside of true life. The journey of those eighteen inches between our head and heart is where so many of us get sidelined in our experience of transformation. At some point we have to accept with our heart the mystery of love's power.

When the apostle Paul wrote the believers at Ephesus, he pled with them to know the love of God personally:

> I pray that out of his glorious riches he may strengthen
> you with power through his Spirit in your inner being,
> so that Christ may dwell in your hearts through faith.
> And I pray that you, being rooted and established in

love, may have power, together with all the saints, to
grasp how wide and long and high and deep is the love
of Christ, *and to know this love that surpasses knowledge.*
(Eph. 3:16–19)

Paul wants us to experience God's love—not just study it or hear
about it. We need to taste it for ourselves. We need to feel our own hearts
swell inside to know that God loves us as Jesus loved Lazarus. Knowing
love personally is different from reading about it. We can have a wealth
of knowledge and yet remain unmoved, unalive, and unaltered. Paul
knew this all too well because his years of trying to please God as a
Pharisee sucked the very life out of him—as human effort always will.
Now Paul tells us that love *surpasses* knowledge. Sacred Love cannot be
explained. It can only be experienced.

As I write this, my wife and I are at the North Carolina coast for a
few days of rest. Our son, Jordan, came to be with us and brought his
girlfriend for us to meet. Jordan and Sara have been dating for several
months but this is the first time we've seen the two of them together.
Jordan is different. He is smitten with his love for Sara. He is acting
with a tenderness and gentleness that seems odd for an Army officer on
his way to fight in Iraq. Jordan told us that he left his Army base, prior
to coming to the beach, to drive two hours to Atlanta to buy an engagement ring for Sara. It's fun to see our son changed so dramatically by
love. Love does this to a person. The smitten heart—is there any rival
force on earth?

When we are smitten by the love of God, we do not remain the
same. This amazing love changes us from the inside out. We lay down

our efforts to understand exactly why this is true. It is an even deeper mystery than the change we know when we fall in love with another person. Human love has a power of its own to get people to do strange things, but only Sacred Love brings the life you and I need.

It was God's Voice of Love that changed Jesus' life as well. Earlier in Jesus' life He was in the waters about to be baptized by His cousin, John the Baptist. Mark tells us that during the baptism, the clouds were being torn back one cumulus cloud after another. Divine Love was moving, and the clouds were in the way. Love could not contain itself. Love spoke and the heavens were "torn open" (Mark 1:10). Jesus and all those standing around heard these words, "You are my Son, whom I love; with you I am well pleased" (Mark 1:11). Love spoke and the entire trajectory of Jesus' life changed—after that day the public ministry of Jesus of Nazareth began.

When we know our true identity as the Beloved of God, we awaken to the life that we were created to live. It is a life God passionately wants us to live. At the tomb of Lazarus, we see that love compels Jesus to initiate. This same love will make Lazarus respond. This is what love does. It makes us move away from death to life. It causes us to move, to change, to transform. Without the personal experience of this love, we will remain the same.

TRANSFORMING YOUR OWN SOUL-SICKNESS

I studied the love of God in Bible studies in college. I learned the Greek and Hebrew words for God's love in seminary. I preached on the love of God as a pastor. I found it natural to speak of the love of

God to others. But when the crowds had gone away, I wondered how God could really love *me*. I saw how God loved others who were more gifted, more talented, more physically attractive—even those who had more hair. But when I looked in the mirror, I could not picture myself as God's beloved.

This became a cancer of the soul, eating away at me for years. It undermined my life—relationships, jobs, everything. I felt I had to prove myself to be loveable, while deep inside I really hated myself. This need to make myself loveable proved to be a significant contributor to the deterioration of my family life that I described earlier. My position made me feel more loved, more identified, and more known than the love of God did. It was not until I knew myself to be the Beloved of God—singled out as a soul-sick man in his forties—that I began to be transformed.

The seed of transformation that took root in my life was this: I had to learn to accept being accepted. I had to *be* loved. For me this meant coming to grips with the unconditional love of God for me alone, not the world. I could more easily understand the love of God for the world than for myself.

Perhaps Lazarus had this same dilemma. He had seen Jesus in action, witnessed His miracles, heard His words, but until Jesus stood in front of that tomb, calling his own name out, he had missed what he needed most to live as Jesus intended. Lazarus could not taste for himself the transforming power of God until Jesus spoke to him in the tomb.

It is so much easier to tell others that God loves them than to believe in our own hearts, *God loves me!* Yet unless God's love becomes personal to us, we will never be able to experience authentic transformation because we won't believe that God is able to transform *us* into who He created us to be as individuals. This kind of love simply says, "I matter and you matter too!" This kind of love is irresistible and contagious.

Until we realize that Jesus is willing and able to come to our own tombs and speak words of love, we will live a lie. In our churches we will stand and sing of God's love and the life that Jesus offers, but inside we will stand alone in fear that He may not call our name out as He called the name of Lazarus. This kind of lie robs us of the life Jesus wants for us—a life in which we enjoy the love of a God who would do anything to free us.

GOD'S COMMAND TO LOVE

I recently led a retreat on being the Beloved of God. Shortly after my talk a man approached me red-faced, almost charging through the people who were waiting patiently to share their thoughts with me.

"I came here to get my butt kicked by Jesus," he said, "not to be made to feel good about myself. I'm sick and tired of this feel-good stuff. I want the truth!"

I wept inside, for this man had been conditioned to believe that to be close to God, he needed to feel guilty. Unless he felt condemned, he didn't feel close to God. He didn't want to hear the real truth about his worth—he was fearfully and wonderfully made—or about how desirable he was to God. For years he had heard teaching about an angry, disappointed heavenly Father whom he could never quite please, no matter how much he accomplished.

We have relaxed the tension between self-denial and self-love too much in our Christian culture. It seems we have no room to walk across the great expanse of these two central teachings of the Christian faith. Paul's plea in Galatians 5:14, "Love your neighbor as *yourself*," is called the *whole law*. Complete.

We learn to let ourselves be loved when we learn to hear God's voice. But the whole idea of loving ourselves often makes us uncomfortable. Loving ourselves seems to contradict Jesus' teachings about self-denial. For example: "If anyone would come after me, he must deny himself" (Matt. 16:24). "If anyone comes to me and does not hate … even his own life—he cannot be my disciple" (Luke 14:26). As Walter Trobisch, a Swiss counselor and writer, expressed, "Indeed we are so ingrained with the idea of self-denial, self-sacrifice, and the fear of being egotistical that the admonition to love one's self seems almost a blasphemy."[3]

Allowing yourself to be loved is not a human blasphemy. Quite the contrary. Rejecting this love is what goes against the teachings of Jesus. Jesus does not call us to focus only on ourselves, but He does call us to know our incredible worth to God and live out of that understanding. He calls us to believe that nothing we can do will ever make God love us more or less than He does right now. This runs contrary to our "do more, do it better" culture. As the priest and writer Henri Nouwen says:

> Yes, there is that voice, the voice that speaks from above and from within and that whispers softly or declares loudly: "You are my Beloved, on you my favor rests." It certainly is not easy to hear that voice in a world

filled with voices that shout: "You are no good, you
are ugly; you are worthless; you are despicable, you are
nobody—unless you can demonstrate the opposite."
These negative voices are so loud and so persistent that
it is easy to believe them.[4]

If we live believing that God is always angry, annoyed, or disap-
pointed with us, we will never hear his voice calling us from the tomb.
We may lift up our heads off the cold slabs we call home, but we say,
"No. Jesus couldn't be calling me. It must be someone else." Negative
voices jeer, "You can't." "You aren't." "You don't have what it takes."
Their seductive power woos us to stay "safe" inside the tomb.

Now listen to Jesus' invitation of love to you:

> Are you tired? Worn out? Burned out on religion?
> Come to me. Get away with me and you'll recover your
> life. I'll show you how to take a real rest. Walk with
> me and work with me—watch how I do it. Learn the
> unforced rhythms of grace. I won't lay anything heavy
> or ill-fitting on you. Keep company with me and you'll
> learn to live freely and lightly. (Matt. 11:28–30 MSG)

These are the words we need to sit with and listen to. These are
words that speak the language we recognize: Recover your life. Take
a real rest. Watch how I do it. And especially: Live freely and lightly.
These are words of love, are they not? These are the words of invitation
to come to Jesus. Yet in our sophisticated world of obligation, do we

discern the difference between coming to Jesus and coming to a meeting? Realizing what it means to truly experience Jesus is also a part of transformation.

When we are worn out by our own attempts to change a habit, it's time for Jesus to show us the way. When Jesus says, "Walk with me and work with me," we hear the invitation of a loving God Who says, "Okay. You've tried it your way. Now try it my way."

Henri Nouwen goes on to write, "I have come to realize that the greatest trap in our life is not success, popularity, or power, but self-rejection.… Self-rejection is the greatest enemy of the spiritual life because it contradicts the sacred voice that calls us the 'Beloved.' Being the Beloved expresses the core truth of our existence."[5]

Transforming love gives us the security to really *live*! It reminds us of our true identity as children of God. The Beloved of God. It reminds us that we can do *nothing* to manufacture God's love for us. From this secure foundation we can love others well, just as a child who knows love at home expresses joy and freedom in her interactions with others. When we recognize how much God loves us, we are recognizing who He created us to be.

WITH GOD ON OUR SIDE

Jesus was determined that not even death would separate him from the love He had for Lazarus. Paul reminds us that nothing can "separate us from the love of Christ" (Rom. 8:39). Nothing!

Paul elaborates in this famous Romans 8 text when he mentions a few wild, untamed forces that we might think could castrate love's power:

The One who died for us—who was raised to life for us!—is in the presence of God at this very moment sticking up for us. Do you think anyone is going to be able to drive a wedge between us and Christ's love for us? There is no way! Not trouble, not hard times, not hatred, not hunger, not homelessness, not bullying threats, not backstabbing, not even the worst sins listed in Scripture…. *None of this fazes us because Jesus loves us.* I'm absolutely convinced that nothing—nothing living or dead, angelic or demonic, today or tomorrow, high or low, thinkable or unthinkable—*absolutely nothing can get between us and God's love because of the way that Jesus our Master has embraced us.* (Rom. 8:34–39 msg)

Take a moment and read Paul's words again. This time, think of a threatening power that you are experiencing right now or perhaps a force that seems to have gripped someone you love. What kind of trouble is in your mind? What hard time are you in right now? What threat are you facing? What seems to be getting between you and God's love?

Pause again and hear the Voice of Love calling you. The greater voice of love is more powerful than what is tormenting you. This Sacred Love expressed through the voice of Jesus is the strongest force we have ever seen. David Benner tells us, "Gravity may hold planets in orbit and nuclear force may hold the atom together, but only love has the power to transform persons."[6] Someone to love us. Someone to fight for us. Someone to be "for" us and not against us. Someone to come get us out. Someone who demonstrates that we matter. Someone who says, "I want you. I accept you as you are. I am here for you. Let's move forward." When Jesus spoke those three all important words to Lazarus—"Lazarus, come forth!"—He was demonstrating that He was for Lazarus. This is what this love does. Sacred Love announces to us time and time again that God is for us.

Until we experience the power of Sacred Love, we will run to anyone who promises to give it; try anything we can to experience it; hold anyone or anything so that we can feel it. But in the end we come back to the same realization that God's love alone frees us to change.

LEARNING TO LISTEN TO THE VOICE OF LOVE

In that significant tomb time of my life, my days had become so busy that I felt like I had become a hamster on a spinning wheel and could not get off. I thought that the spinning life was life indeed. I did not know I had an alternative. I did not know the life that Jesus promised. A sincere friend confronted me with the truth: Steve, you are a man striving, striving to be loved. If I did well, I would be loved. If I did the spectacular things, then I would be loved. It was a life of "ifs." If I would do this, then … If I would do that, then …

My journey out of the tomb of busyness and isolation began with learning the two most unnatural activities for an extrovert: Be silent and experience solitude. During my time at the monastery, I was forced to become a "recovering extrovert"—a person who sought to live a life in rhythm between being with others and being alone, being active, and being quiet.

In a quiet place I became aware of how noisy my heart really was. I kept hearing something that went like this: *This is a waste of time. You could be doing so much more if you would just go home.* And the big one was: *You paid for this experience?* It took time and practice to quiet my noisy inner and outer worlds. Yet soon I began to prefer the alone times of my life more than grilling hamburgers for parties on my deck at home.

Silence and solitude became the tools of transformation for me to hear what my soul-sick soul needed to hear: I am loved. I am wanted. I am the object of Jesus' love. I could not hear this through my activities. I could not hear in any other way except to pull away to lonely places and to listen for Jesus to speak *my* name out of the 6.6 billion people on the planet: "*Steve*, come forth."

When I finally heard Jesus' Voice of Love, I realized I did not need to do all I was doing to gain approval. I saw, for the first time, how my quest for acceptance kept me from fully loving my family. My world had become one filled with obligation, not joy, because I was doing it for an elusive applause rather than out of my love for others.

Paul tells us in Ephesians 1:4–6 (MSG):

> Long before he laid down earth's foundations, he had us in mind, *had settled on us as the focus of his love*, to be made whole and holy by his love. Long, long ago he decided to adopt us into his family through Jesus Christ. (What pleasure he took in planning this!) He wanted us to enter into the celebration of his lavish gift-giving by the hand of his beloved Son.

Transformation is the journey to be made "whole and holy by his love." These are the twin desires of every Christ-follower of every age. This journey is not based on human effort but on being loved deeply by God. This is the root that grows a flourishing life that goes on to experience transformation, not just once but continually.

No other religion offers a love that is not dependent on what we do. As popular contemporary Christian author Philip Yancey writes, "The Buddhist eight-fold path, the Hindu doctrine of karma, the Jewish covenant, and Muslim code of law—each of these offers a way to earn approval. Only Christianity dares to make God's love unconditional."[7]

My instruction in listening to Jesus' love started when I began pouring out my story to Dallas Willard at the monastery. After gently listening, he said, "Steve, I'd like to ask you to make a commitment to only read the words of Jesus—just the 'red letters'—and nothing else for the next two years. Furthermore I'd like to ask you to only preach the words of Jesus. Not Paul. Not Peter. Not David, Moses, or any of the prophets. Only Jesus."

I would have normally argued with someone asking me to do such a thing. After all, the *whole* Bible is God's Word. But this was not a time to argue. When you're broken, you're broken. I did what I was encouraged to do.

I bought a "red-letter edition" of the Bible, and it has become one of the best investments I've ever made for my soul. For the next two years I simply read what Jesus said. I began with Matthew and listened as each red consonant and vowel formed words—words of life. With the turn of each page, I began to feel myself coming to life again. When I read about Jesus delighting in those He loved, I felt joy—that "exuberance for life."[8]

When I read about the disciples being in the storm-tossed boat in Mark 4, I felt that Jesus was entering the storm-tossed and sinking boat and staying *with me*. My simple prayer became, "Jesus, be in my boat." I became more God-aware and at the same time, more self-aware, and through this became more alive than I had ever been before.

And so one of the most precious gifts I received during my time in the monastery was learning how to hear the Voice of Jesus. "Lazarus, come forth!" Lazarus heard and the dead man was transformed. "Steve, come forth!" I heard and I began my journey toward being transformed.

I was dead, like Lazarus, but listening to the Voice of Jesus began to slowly resurrect my soul. I heard not condemnation or anger or shame. I heard an invitation. It was an invitation to become my true self. My many false selves had to stay in the tomb. It was my true self that Jesus loved so deeply. It was my true self that needed to live. Perhaps yours does as well.

RECOGNIZING THE VOICE OF LOVE

Do we hear the voice of God in our Christian communities? If we don't, we will find ourselves sitting in church pews week after week, month after month, and year after year waiting to hear a loving word—any word that can bring life. We will settle into a false belief that says, "So this is it. This is the life Jesus spoke about." Maybe we have missed something. I think many of us have.

Saint Anthony was once asked how he differentiated between angels who came to him humble and devils who came in rich disguise. He said you could tell by how he felt after they had departed. When an angel left him, he felt strengthened by his presence. When a devil left, he felt horror. What if we applied this test to the voices heard today in our pulpits and programs, from our colleagues and classes?

My wife and I recently attended a church worship service at the urging of friends. We had been invited to visit this particular church because of the preacher's "amazing ability to preach heaven down." Since I'm always interested in hearing good preaching and teaching, we went. What we heard was judgment—not life. What we felt was shame, not grace. We left the building, sorry for ourselves and burdened for the people who had equated deafening, boisterous, forceful, guilt-producing words with the loving voice of God.

Just before John tells us the story about Lazarus, he tells us what Jesus said about how to listen to his voice—the voice of the Good Shepherd:

> The sheep *recognize* his voice. He *calls his own sheep by name* and leads them out. When he gets them all out, he leads them and they follow *because they are familiar with his voice.* They won't follow a stranger's voice but will scatter because they aren't used to the sound of it. (John 10:3–5 MSG)

Jesus says it in a simple way that is easy to understand. We can recognize Jesus' voice because it is the Voice of Love that breathes life into us. Other voices might masquerade as Jesus, but if they are not life-giving, they are not from God. Jesus' Voice leads us out of the tomb and into life. As we get to know the Voice of Jesus, it becomes easier to discern when He is speaking. We accumulate experiences that show that only listening to love allows us to come alive.

This image of the shepherd helps us understand God's heart for us. Yet upon hearing this new teaching, many of the people became upset and said, "Why listen to him?" (John 10:20). People in every generation are still asking this question. *Why listen to Jesus? Why not other leaders? What does Jesus say that is so different?*

In fact, when was the last time you attended a seminar on "How to Listen to Jesus"? Classes are designed for us to listen to a *teacher*. Sermons are written and delivered for us to listen to the *preacher*. There is no shortage of powerful, charismatic, and influential voices out there today, all eager to get us to listen to them. But in the end these powerful voices—whether from preachers or politicians—can only speak with voices that are as horizontal, flat, and as merely human as our own. Human words without the inspiration of the vertical influence of God simply cannot bring transformation. Mere mortals can offer advice, impart motivation, and cast vision, but their words alone will not ignite change in us that will last for eternity. We need the words of God.

LISTENING MEANS NOTICING

I don't know exactly what a prayer is.
I do know how to pay attention....
—Mary Oliver

Luke records the story of Jesus hiking through the mountains one day, along with his three climbing companions: Peter, James, and John (the same John who wrote about Lazarus). As these three ordinary men reached the top, God chose to elevate Jesus above the status of Moses and Elijah. Luke says it happened this way: "A voice came from the cloud, saying 'This is my Son, whom I have chosen: *listen* to him'" (Luke 9:35).

When God spoke at the beginning of the world, creation and life came into existence. When Jesus spoke to Lazarus, new life emerged. No wonder God is passionate for us to listen to Jesus. As Peter asked Jesus once when others were walking away: "'Lord, to whom shall we go? You have the words of eternal life'" (John 6:68). Peter's realization becomes our invitation to allow the words of Jesus to breathe life into us now—no matter what our condition.

What does it mean to listen to God's Voice of Love in everyday life? Gwen and I often use the story of Moses in Exodus 3:1–6 to help others learn to discern God's voice amid all the other voices competing for our attention.

On a very ordinary day Moses is leading his father-in-law's flock to the backside of Horeb, the mountain of God. And then he *noticed* something—a burning bush that was not consumed. As he paid attention to what he was seeing, something very significant happened. God spoke.

Let's look at this more closely. We read, "Moses saw that though the bush was on fire it did not burn up. So Moses thought, 'I will go over and see this strange sight—why the bush does not burn up'" (Ex. 3:2–3).

Had Moses not noticed the burning bush, he would have missed the greatest revelation of God's identity known in the history of the Jews.

God was waiting on Moses to see beyond the bush and to enter the mystery of what was about to happen. All of this happened because Moses noticed something. As Moses became curious and moved toward the bush, God revealed His name—and no one had ever heard or known the name of God before this time.[9]

When Moses noticed the bush, his attention shifted from bleating sheep and cud-chewing cows to the sacred. Even the ground felt different. Poet and author David Whyte reminds us that this experience for Moses meant more than the opening of his eyes:

> It is Moses in the desert
> Fallen to his knees before the lit bush.
> It is the man throwing away his shoes
> As if to enter heaven
> And finding himself astonished,
> Opened at last,
> Fallen in love with solid ground.[10]

When we are intentional about noticing our relational and physical surroundings, we see things we did not see before. Jesus encouraged us to "notice" when he reminded us to look at the birds and to observe the flowers (Matt. 6:25–34). The simplicity of a wildflower reveals the effortless care that God offers us. A western bluebird landing on a golden Aspen branch reveals the loving faithfulness of God. Referring to this passage, Martin Luther tells us that there are times in our spiritual journey when "birds should be our teachers and flowers our theologians."

We will not notice the birds or flowers around us if we succumb to the busyness of our culture. In other words, when we move too quickly, we cannot hear the Voice of Love. We dispel information about God rather than inviting people to experience God. We major on tips and techniques rather than allowing people to taste the mystery of God's presence. We are talked at and preached to rather than invited to "taste and see that the Lord is good" (Ps. 34:8). Our busyness annihilates our hearts[11] and worship feels empty or manipulated, not Spirit-driven. When this happens, we are more in the tomb than out of it.

What would it look like if small group gatherings, casual conversations, and dinner tables were places where people could share what they "noticed" about God during their week? A great question to begin a time together in almost any setting is: How did you experience God's love this past week? What has God been saying to you lately?

The ancient spiritual exercises also help us learn how to enter silence and be alone with ourselves. There our aloneness is transformed to true solitude. We find that we are at last at home with ourselves and experience peace with God.

In my own life I am learning to hear from God what I have tried to hear from my father. God also uses other loving voices to speak His words of love. Teachers, coaches, mentors, parents, grandparents, friends, and spouses can all speak the language of the Voice of Love to all of us. The fact is we need many voices speaking this same life-giving language for us to navigate our way out of the tombs. God used my son Blake to awaken me to my busyness, for instance, and a friend who told me of the monastery in California and said, "Steve, here is something you need to do and do it quick."

Learning to notice Jesus' voice in ordinary ways every day will help us discern when someone is speaking true words of loving correction or affirmation, or debilitating words of false condemnation. We also need to explore ways that each of us can speak words of truth and love to one another to help encourage each other on the journey. We must always come back to Jesus' voice because only His voice will tell us our true identity.

CALLING YOUR NAME

Pause for a moment now and imagine what Jesus thinks about you. Imagine Jesus finding you in the midst of a crowd that is following Him and motioning with His hand for you to come and walk in private with Him. Perhaps at first you can't imagine that Jesus would single you out of the crowd and motion for you to come to Him. But Jesus makes it clear, even in your disbelief, that He wants time with you. As you walk toward Him, what do you hear Him say to you?

I've found many people are uncomfortable in doing this exercise. Many of us, when trying to describe what Jesus might speak to our ears alone might share *any* feeling but love. People have shared with me that "Jesus feels disappointment when he thinks of me." One woman told me, "Jesus would not even want to speak to me because I had an abortion when I was in college. Now all I feel is guilt and shame, and I know Jesus wants me to feel guilty all the time because of what I did."

David Benner reminds us, "Regardless of what you have come to believe about God based on your life experience, the truth is that when God thinks of you, love swells in his heart and a smile comes to his face."[12] Do you believe this? Are you ready to respond to the Voice of Love calling your name?

Imagine yourself, in the midst of your own tomb surrounded by sealed walls and no way out, hearing a voice calling you to come forth! A power beyond the tomb's walls calling you to leave the tomb and to embrace what lies ahead.

John tells us that Jesus cried (11:35) and was deeply moved (11:33, 38) knowing His friend was in a tomb where His own arms could not embrace him. And so He walked toward the tomb. He called the name of His beloved friend unashamedly.

Loudly.

Boldly.

Gallantly.

The Voice of Love defied the tomb to hold him any longer. The one who Jesus loved had lost all hope. But as the Voice of Love reminded the crowd that day, the end is never the end when Jesus shows up.

NOTES

[1] David G. Benner, *Surrender to Love* (Downers Grove, IL: IVP, 2003), 11.

[2] Dr. Bill Leonard in "Transforming Ministry for a Changing World." Wake Forest Divinity School Bulletin 2007–2008, 1.

[3] Walter Trobisch, *Love Yourself* (Downers Grove, IL: IVP, 1976), 14.

4 Henri Nouwen, *Life of the Beloved* (New York: Crossroad, 1995), 27.

5 Nouwen, *Life of the Beloved,* 27.

6 Benner, *Surrender to Love,* 10.

7 Philip Yancey, *What's So Amazing About Grace?* (Grand Rapids, MI.: Zondervan, 1997), 45.

8 I would strongly suggest that you read Paul's list of the "fruit of the Spirit" in *The Message* in Galatians 5:22-23. This is the kind of transformation that God longs to offer us. If we are not experiencing this kind of fruit—we need transformation. Paul's words, expressed so masterfully in Eugene Peterson's work, help us realize the real, authentic goal of a transformed life.

9 See Exodus 3:1-15 for the entire account of this fascinating story. God offers his name to Moses and to us because Moses "turned aside."

10 David Whyte, "The Opening of Eyes" in *River Flow: New & Selected Poems 1984-2007* (Langley, WA: Many Rivers Press, 2007), 31.

11 The meaning of "busyness" in Chinese is composed of two words: heart and annihilation.

12 Benner, *Surrender to Love,* 16.

Chapter Five

THE STENCH OF TRANSFORMATION:

THE MESSY REALITIES OF SPIRITUAL CHANGE

"By this time there is a bad odor,
for he has been there four days."

—John 11:39

- Sometimes, transformation stinks.
- Many people don't know this and so they knowingly or unknowingly reject the person in the midst of transformation.
- True transformation happens when we expose the stench of our sins and shames to God.
- Even when others turn away, Jesus stays with us.

So finally Jesus was there. Jesus spoke. Mary and Martha, who waited and prayed and anguished, had the hope again of embracing their brother. Yet when Jesus asked for the tomb to be opened, Martha objected: "But Lord … by this time there is a bad odor, for he has been there four days" (vs. 39). She knew what we know. Dead things smell. She wanted change, but she wanted it in a certain way.

Just like Martha, when we realize that something has to change and actually *could* change, we want the change to happen quickly and neatly. But transformation is rarely quick or neat. Lazarus's story is a beautiful, messy reminder of this.

Many of the artists who took brush to canvas reveal the stinking realities of Lazarus's transformation. Take a moment and look at the Giotto print on the inside front cover. Can you make out the veiled women standing near the tomb's entrance pulling their clothes over their noses? How about the other observers standing near the tomb, retreating from their front-row view of the resurrection? It was simply too much. After all, as the tomb of Lazarus was opened, four days of death's decay revealed its ugly fruit. We don't like to think about the real facts associated with Lazarus's transformation. But make no mistake, as Giotto and other painters from various centuries all intuited: Sometimes transformation stinks.

When we emerge from our tombs, we also reek with odor—that's what transformation is like when we first face our circumstances and soul-sickness. The smell and messiness often repel onlookers, leaving us feeling lonely and rejected. This can be particularly difficult to accept because we have been so excited about hearing the voice of love call us from the tomb. It's hard to remember that God's call is the wonderful *beginning* to a lifetime of transformation, a lifetime of hearing His voice of love heal us from a specific sin, shame, or circumstance of our life. We might find complete freedom from certain trappings in this life, and we will certainly have "aha" moments on our spiritual journey, but we cannot predict the course of our transformation.

The smell of Lazarus's body reeks of the reality of his physical tomb—and reminds us that God is able to transform anyone at any time in any circumstance! With this hope in mind, why do we keep forgetting that in the process of transformation, ugly smells might have to come out in the open?

Transformation in the spiritual life involves death—death to self, death to the past, death to the dreams we once dreamed apart from God. In the midst of the stink of our lives, we press on because we know that death is the step before resurrection.

A MESSY PROCESS

My friend Thomas used to work on a property management team for an apartment complex. One day his colleagues dropped him off at a vacated apartment that was going to be rented out again. His boss told him, "Just get rid of the smell. We'll be back in five hours."

The apartment had been home to numerous cats, five dogs, and a series of parties involving heavy drug use. The tenants had finally been evicted after the utilities had been turned off, and they had apparently left the apartment in a fit of resentment. Trash on the floor, dirty clothes left behind, holes in the walls, dog-doo on the carpet, urine stains on the hardwood.

It took Thomas two hours to work his way back to the kitchen. He cleaned the sink, threw out the boxes of food in the cabinets, and opened the fridge—and started gagging from the assault of a fetid green and purple stench. He stepped back as if punched in the gut and quickly shut the door. The tenants had left food in the fridge. The power had then been turned off and the food sat there for weeks, rotting.

Thomas went outside to sit down and get some air. To literally take a breather. He then went back in and took one thing out of the fridge and threw it in a trash bag. Shut the fridge again and took another breather. The smell was so bad he couldn't stand it for more than two minutes. The next time he went back, it was a little easier to breathe and he slowly removed all of the disgusting, rotting food, one thing at a time. Then he sprayed down the shelves with bleach, wiped everything one more time, and left the fridge door propped open so that air could get in.

This is how the transformation of a person works. We have to get rid of the things that smell and are in need of change, one item at a time. (We'll explore specific ways to get rid of smelly things in chapter 7.) Ignoring the stench of what has gone foul in our lives will not alleviate the odor; it will make us sick.

In my role as a spiritual director, I had the opportunity to meet with a woman who served as a missionary in Africa. She told me that her grandfather had sexually abused her from age four to eight. She'd shelved and suppressed these memories for many years and had hoped they were in the past. But soon into her marriage with the stress of children and cross-culture living, the past broke out and the stink surfaced and washed over her, making her feel like a hopeless victim.

Her mission agency did not explore this issue with her prior to her becoming a missionary. She did not tell them. Her sending churches did not know about this issue. She secretly carried the smelly, foul stench of sexual abuse for decades. The smell had made her marriage toxic and poisoned her soul.

She told me, "I have to talk about this with someone who is safe. Can you help me?" We spent hours unpacking her story chapter by chapter. Over time we worked together to clean out the rotten stench of her abuse. She sensed God's healing, and the power of resurrection was breathed back into her and her marriage. She would not remain in the stink forever. But there was no substitute for the hours we spent together talking through these deep issues, cleaning out shelf after shelf of filth. As a result of her commitment to the transformation process, today she is a stronger person and more alive as she walks toward Jesus.

LOOKING FOR THE SOURCE

Many of us have seen Old Faithful in Yellowstone National Park. Every hour or so, this gigantic geyser spews water and steam high into the air as a result of internal pressure building up below the earth's surface. Below the ground, where the eye cannot see, is natural piping that the water has channeled into the soft stone. If you walk by Old Faithful when it's not spewing and sputtering, you wouldn't know that thousands of gallons of steaming hot water are underneath the surface. You would simply see a hole in the ground.

This is a helpful image of the sin and pain in our lives that erupts on a regular basis. Until we look below the surface, we will settle for trying to control the flow of water to make it less messy; remember Willard's phrase—"sin management"? Real transformation requires tracing the hidden piping to the vast reservoirs that have held the water for years. Only then can we do something about the source of the eruptions.

For instance, learning to control anger requires more than counting to ten and trying not to think about whatever makes you angry. This journey requires an in-depth, slow process of exploring reasons for unhealthy anger in the first place. *What am I desiring when I act in rage? What would it look like to acknowledge my feelings without lashing out at someone? What am I really angry about that I'm not addressing? What am I longing for?* Find that reservoir and you'll find the way to be transformed. Greed, food addiction, selfishness, alcoholism, and more all work in a similar way. Something deeper than is visible to the eye is causing us to fall into the same habits again and again.

Jason called me one day from another state to tell me he was in trouble. He asked if he could come visit for a few days. As his story unfolded, I learned that Jason had gotten involved in an emotional affair with one of his staff. His marriage was running on empty, and this new relationship promised a love like he had always envisioned. He considered leaving his wife and kids.

As we talked for hours, it became clear that this woman was offering Jason loving words, promises, and escape. That's exactly what he wanted. But the word got out at home, church, and office. Carnage. Mess. Stink.

Jason's journey is now walking the long journey back into his past to better understand some of his own wounds in growing up. He now regrets substituting the love of this emotional affair for the unconditional love he has been seeking all along. Jason is doing exactly what Paul describes in 2 Corinthians 7:9–11 (MSG):

You were jarred into turning things around. You let the
distress bring you to God, not drive you from him. The
result was all gain, no loss. Distress that drives us to
God does that. It turns us around. It gets us back in the
way of salvation. We never regret that kind of pain.…
And now isn't it wonderful all the ways in which this
distress has goaded you closer to God? You're more
alive, more concerned, more sensitive, more reverent,
more human, more passionate, more responsible.

Paul is describing a journey of transformation. It often begins with
some kind of "jarring" that reveals how much we smell. But notice all
the things Paul describes that happen when we get "turned around."
We become more alive, more concerned, more of all that we really want
in life. This is important for us to reflect on at times when jarring happens. It's not the end. Transformation is beginning and it continues
throughout our journey.

This jarring experience, though messy and smelly, is helping to
turn Jason's life around. He is on the road now to authentic transformation. Jason wants all of Paul's words. Every description of life, he
wants for himself. This is what awaits us as we transform. Not only
for Jason, but for you and me.

THEN THE CLEANIN'

The first church I pastored was in the beautiful hills of Kentucky. The
community of people there loved the great farmlands and streams and

rivers that abounded everywhere. One Saturday afternoon a wise, older deacon took me out fishing. I was young, still in seminary, and obviously green. This deacon wanted to teach me a few things he felt I needed to know about being a pastor. The fishing trip was to be my classroom.

Sitting on the banks of that Kentucky lake surrounded by bluegrass and bluegills, the deacon told me something I have never forgotten. "Steve, preachin' is like fishin'. First you catch 'em. Then you clean 'em." It made sense to me at the time. In fact it sounded as easy as 1, 2, 3. Years later I don't dismiss the deacon's wisdom, but I do believe it comes up short. What I have learned is that, yes, first you catch 'em. But the cleaning? It's far from easy. It takes a lifetime. I see this in my own life as much as in the lives of others.

I remember one instance when the smelliness and slowness of my own transformation particularly surprised me. On my fortieth birthday my wife planned a lavish party at a clubhouse. We gathered for food and enjoyed fun, fellowship, and frolic. After the party I went to my bookshelf and pulled out all of the journals that I had used to plot my journey. Since becoming a Christian in college, I was encouraged to keep a written record of my life—a sort of memoir in the making. These spiral-bound, ragged-edged journals contained my own private psalms through which I'd often cry out for God to change me.

I was not prepared for what I read on the eve of my journey into the next decade of life. As I flipped through the pages, I realized that many of the issues I struggled with in college were still plaguing me twenty years later. Since college I had made many efforts to change. But even after all the books I'd read, seminars I'd attended, sermons I'd heard, and small group studies I'd experienced, I still found dark places in my soul that needed Jesus. It saddened and disturbed me that midway through my spiritual journey, I still needed to be transformed.

It's one thing *to become* a Christian. To *be* a Christian is more challenging. To be a Christian means to be continually involved in the transformation process. We never get to quit changing. If we quit changing, we're spiritually dead. If we quit changing, we're finished. We're done. We never stop transforming in the spiritual life. The cleaning takes a lifetime.

You and I are morphing into the image God had in mind all along. One day we will be free from the messes of earthly lives. Lazarus's story reminds us that living as a Christian now requires *ongoing* transformation.

The reality of my need for transformation no longer surprises me. I know that when I am aware of how messy my spiritual life can be, I am aware of my need for Jesus. Only then can I be alert to how He is going to change me for His glory alone.

A SAFE PLACE

Perhaps the reason so few of us experience authentic transformation is that we do not feel safe enough to experience a soul cleansing in specific areas of our lives that smell the worst. When the writers of the New Testament refer to sin in our lives, they usually refer to black-and-white issues.[1] We often refer to the sin in our lives without owning and confessing the specific issues that get us into trouble. When we are unclear about what it is that we are being transformed *from*, we lose sight of why we need transformation so desperately. Without a safe place to speak of these specific struggles, we will not find true transformation.

Consider Bill who, like most of us, has struggled with one sin more than others most of his life. Yet through years of small groups and amicable relationships, no one around Bill ever really knew what Bill was struggling with. He asked for prayer from his friends but never gave specific information or elaborated. He never felt comfortable enough with people to tell them the whole truth. Over the years, he became good at denying the sin even to himself. Now, in his fifties, Bill is finally opening up to a few friends about his problem. Why now? Because Bill got caught at work viewing Internet pornography, and the word got out. Ashamed and yet a little relieved, Bill looked to his church to support him as he sought counseling for the first time. However, his pastor and small group didn't know what to do with him. He became a topic of gossip rather than prayer. Embarrassed and broken, Bill and his wife moved away to find solace and get the help he needed. They needed a safe place to be transformed.

A person who seeks an antiseptic, hospital-clean, sterile environment for transformation should not look to Christianity for answers. Jesus himself reminded us that "It is not the healthy who need a doctor. It's the sick" (Matt. 9:12). Sick people—people in need of transformation—need a place to be healed, and most often these places are filled with the odors of all the rotten things that have been happening in people's tombs, whether those things are a result of personal sin, the sins of others, or simply the circumstances of life.

A youth pastor I know was confronted by angry parents when

they realized that their son was not changing fast enough in the youth group. The son had taken a wayward journey into drinking heavily and was experimenting with drugs. The parents suspected that the son had been having sexual escapades as well. The family had joined this particular church because of the reputation of the youth pastor and the youth ministry. The parents made an appointment with the youth pastor to express their frustration over their son's progress or lack of it. The youth pastor gave the parents a forthright answer: "I can't fix in three weeks what your son has messed up in eighteen years." They were stunned and left the church. The parents had to face the *slowness* that we all face on the journey toward transformation.

Our spiritual faith is an earthly, bodily, organic, unrefined journey toward new life. We can't buy it, package it, produce it, or sell it. Perhaps we'd like our faith more if we could get a bottle of Purell, the instant hand-sanitizing liquid that kills 99 percent of germs on contact, and sanitize our sins, our life, our past. But there is no such Purell to buy when it comes to our hearts. Only the slow, smelly work of transformation will heal. This is the Lazarus way. This is the way of authentic change.

THE MESSY CHURCH

We might know this in theory, but in reality most of us in the church prefer stories of dramatic conversions: An alcoholic suddenly finds Jesus, gets baptized, and is free once and for all of the whiskey bottle. A homeless person accepts Christ, puts on the garments of salvation, shaves, and is freed from the grit under his fingernails. A woman who committed adultery for twenty years suddenly realizes the pain she is causing her husband, agrees to never look at another man again, and now enjoys a happy marriage.

Our instant society influences every part of our lives, including the beliefs in our churches. No one wants transformation to take a long time. We want people to find Jesus and get their lives straightened out. We want clean people in unsoiled sanctuaries, singing worship songs in pitch, with no glitches in our PowerPoint, lighting, or microphones.

Transformation does not work like that. Lust does not die in the waters of baptism. Envy does not expire when we accept Jesus as our Savior. Long-suppressed anger does not disappear when we meet Jesus at the front of the church. Nor does greed, overeating, undereating, laziness, or any other stinking reality of earthly life. Let's admit it: You and I still need the ongoing work of Jesus' transforming power.

So why does the church and Christian culture in general rarely acknowledge our stinking condition? Shouldn't there be small groups and classes like this?

- Parents Who Get Too Angry with Their Kids— Chapel, Sundays at 3 p.m.

- Workaholics—Room 105, Thursdays at 5 p.m.

- People Suffering from Panic Attacks—Room 101, Tuesdays at 7 p.m.

- Couples with Sexual Dysfunction—Room 205, Wednesdays at 7 p.m.

- Men Addicted to Porn—Room 103, Tuesdays at 7 p.m.

- Women Who Are Being Abused—Sanctuary,
  Thursdays at 6 p.m.

- Children with Messed-Up Parents—Room 108,
  Sundays at 5 p.m.

- Women Who Have Had an Abortion—Room 3,
  Wednesdays at 4:30 p.m.

- Men Struggling to Live a Heterosexual Life—Room 202,
  Wednesdays at 5 p.m.

- Non-Virgins Preparing for Marriage—Room 101,
  Tuesdays at 8 p.m.

- Parents of Gay Children—Room 109,
  Sundays at 4 p.m.

- Teenagers Who Don't Believe in God—Catacombs,
  Thursdays at 8 p.m.

These are the kinds of topics that people need today. Yet many churches are sadly silent on so many smelly situations that people find themselves stuck in.

A good friend of mine struggles with a smelly addiction. He goes each week to a twelve-step group at a community center. There he sits in a plastic chair in a dimly lit room with linoleum-checkered floors. He meets with the same people, week after week. They sip diluted coffee and eat stale sugar cookies and share their smelly stories of transformation. My friend describes those meetings as if they were the greatest church experience one could ever hope for. Love is present. Acceptance abounds. They have time for every person's story to be heard. My friend has given up on church because he can't find one that offers him the love, acceptance, and safe place to be heard. Too often the church has turned its face away from the smelliness of his emerging life.

FACING REJECTION

When our journey toward wholeness involves the smell of things that need to change, often some form of rejection follows. Jesus did not ask Lazarus to wallow in the stench of transformation. But Lazarus did have to walk through a crowd of people who couldn't take the smell.

Ken is one sad memory I carry in my heart. Ken, who is gay, was a longtime friend of Susan, a woman in a church I pastored. Susan told us about Ken one night in our small group. We all thought our group would be a good place for Ken to explore Christianity, so we invited him to join our group and he came. We were eager to have Ken in our group for the first few meetings.

Then something happened. One couple in our group made an appointment with me privately to voice a concern. "How can we grow as Christians when we have to be so safe for Ken?" they asked me. "Shouldn't Ken be 'put' into another group or even another church?"

The same week, Ken came to me, unknowing that anything was brewing in our group. He wanted to help in the nursery because week after week, he had heard the pleas coming from our children's director: "We need help in the nursery each and every week. Jesus loved children. Won't you come and help us extend the love of Jesus to our children?"

Then chaos ensued. "We can't have a homosexual working in our nursery!" "Steve, you need to do something. Ken is becoming a problem." What I was really being told was, "Steve, take the smelly person outside the church. We are clean in here, and his smell might become too much for us." This story ends on a sad note because Ken got the message and left the church. His curious faith was not welcome where the saints sought to live Pine-Sol lives.

Jesus knew that no smell was more distasteful than the smell of religious people. He saved his harshest criticism for the smelly right wing adherents of the faith.[2] The smell of adultery, theft, swindling, jealousy, doubt, and rejection of faith did not compare in Jesus' heart to the smell of self-righteousness. But true to his way of dealing with smelly people, even those who thought they were spiritually superior to others were welcomed to be in his presence. In the third chapter of John's gospel, we find the story of the Pharisee named Nicodemus.

Seeking the safety of the night's protective air, Nicodemus approached Jesus secretly, perhaps to mask his own smells. Jesus knew that private meetings are sometimes the only place where foul smells can be dealt with. He welcomed Nicodemus and his robes of righteousness. He even welcomed his questions. Jesus made it clear that to live an *alive* life within the Kingdom of God required a process Jesus described as "Being Born Again."

Could Jesus have picked a messier, bloodier image for Christianity? While evangelicals are quick to adopt the language of "being born again," we rarely acknowledge all this implies. Christians are not born clean, warm, and wrapped in white blankets. We are born in the midst of a bloody mess. The good news of Jesus comes to some pretty bad places. For Lazarus, the good news of a second chance at life came to a smelly tomb.

Rather than shake our head in judgment, disbelief, or shame at a foul odor coming from a friend, colleague, or neighbor, we can let the smell serve as a reminder that each of us needs God now. *My friend needs God. God, please help. The stench is really bad. She needs You just as much as I do.*

Jesus does not cover His face when we emerge from the smells of sin and the fumes of failure. He stands ready, waiting, and expectant of such things. So should we.

JESUS' SENSE OF SMELL

Jesus was no stranger to odors that required transformation. It seems, in fact, He had a nose that could sniff out where the work of transformation was needed. The foul stench of a blind man made Jesus stop and heal him. The bad odor of adultery drew Jesus to offer acceptance and healing. The aroma of any secret sin—pride, greed, envy, hatred, jealousy, spiritual arrogance—made Jesus stop in His tracks and speak to the heart of the person harboring the smelly, foul thing.

So Jesus stood at the tomb of Lazarus knowing quite well that the smell would be nauseating. He asked for the stone to be removed. He didn't gag, because He was accustomed to such scents. He did something unexpected. He prayed.

The smell of death motivated Jesus to talk to God—not to turn His head, not to flee, not to make the stench go away. He lifted, not bowed, His head. Perhaps bowing would have looked like He was burying his own nose in His own garments. No, He lifted His head as if to breathe the whole messy stench in more deeply, and He prayed: "Father, I thank you that you have heard me."

John felt it was important to tell us what Jesus said to God. Even when we are in the tomb reeking with this messy life, Jesus prays for us. When we are desperate and lonely and rejected and cry out to God, God does not miss a word. When we remember this, our smell and the smell of others motivates us to ask God for help, not turn our heads.

Jesus loves smelly people. Whether He is talking to Lazarus, Nicodemus, the woman at the well, or *you*, Jesus has a soft spot for people with messy lives.

NOTES

¹ See 1 Cor. 6:9–10, Galatians 5:19–21, and Colossians 3:5–10 as examples of such specific lists of sins.

² Read Jesus' words to the Pharisees in Matthew 23. These are called the "Seven Woes" because Jesus raises seven harsh criticisms of the people who think they are right and righteous before God.

Chapter Six

STEPPING TOWARD LIFE:
CHOOSING TO STUMBLE OUT OF DARKNESS

The dead man came out.

—John 11:43

- Transformation is a step-by-step journey.
- Sometimes stepping into light is unsettling because it is new.
- Transformation is more about ordinary stumbling than dramatic moments.
- The most important thing is to be moving toward Jesus.

One of my favorite hiking trails near our retreat in Colorado is called The Crags. The sign at the trailhead describes what's involved in this particular hike: It has a moderate grade of steepness to it, it will take approximately three hours to do the loop, and dogs must be on a leash at all times. I don't take the time to read the sign now that I've hiked the trail dozens of times. I know what to expect, and I know the exhilarating 360-degree view at the top makes every step worth it.

Gwen and I hike at different speeds. I'm eight inches taller than her so my stride is longer. Before I know it, I'm blazing ahead of her. If I am not careful, a well-intentioned Sunday afternoon hike ends up somewhere between frozen silence and frustrated tears with her feeling I am "not wanting to really 'be' with" her. This makes for an interesting discussion because I thought we were going to conquer a mountain. I forgot we were going to "be" together. See, my heart transformation is still in need in many areas.

The journey toward being a transformed person—the pathway out of the tomb—does not include a map for us to judge our progress or offer a suggested route depending on the length of our stride or strength of our muscles. The story of Lazarus, however, can become a guide to help us find our way. We might be asking, "How long will our transformation take anyway? If we are good 'hikers,' can we finish more quickly?"

John makes a vivid point about Lazarus walking from the tomb into the light of the presence of Jesus: Lazarus was still wrapped in graveclothes. We might want to picture him running to Jesus with open arms, leaping for joy at his resurrection, but Lazarus emerged from the tomb barely able to move at all. He was mummy-like, wobbly, and teeter-tottering like a baby taking first steps in a new life. Yet, while still bound, he moved forward—forward to the Voice of Love that called him. Giotto captures this beautifully in his painting. Take a moment and sit with the image of the bound Lazarus.

This is the same journey each of us must take. Our journey may be one of small stumbles more than dramatic leaps. But on our way to transformation, the most important thing is that *we are moving forward, step-by-step.* We might be bound, but we are standing. We might be halfway between death and life, but we are on our way to Jesus.

ONE MAN'S STORY OF THE STEP-BY-STEP JOURNEY

John Newton's life is a story of this stumbling journey toward transformation. Newton was a captain of a ship in the eighteenth century that transported slaves to the New World in exchange for resources discovered in America. The business was lucrative. The life was wretched.

Aboard the slave ship *Greyhound* on May 12, 1748, in a violent storm at sea, John Newton accepted Jesus Christ as his Savior and his Lord. Yet Newton continued in the slave trade for six more years, sailing back and forth from Africa to the New World exchanging chained souls for kegged rum. The transformation that began with accepting Jesus Christ as his Savior was a long, unsteady process.

In 1764, ten years after giving up his profession and sixteen years after his conversion on the storm-tossed sea, Newton became an Anglican priest. In 1787, thirty-nine years after his conversion to Christianity,

John Newton wrote a tract titled, "Thoughts Upon the African Slave Trade," which greatly aided William Wilberforce, a member of the British parliament, to campaign against slave trading.

John Newton's story can be disturbing for us if we prefer to imagine a slave-trading captain falling to his knees in the bowels of the ship, praying for God's mercy, asking Jesus into his heart, then getting up and unlocking the chains of captured slaves and sailing home in victory. In fact, many years after his conversion, Newton wrote of that time, "I was greatly deficient in many respects.... I cannot consider myself to have been a believer (in the full sense of the word) till a considerable time afterwards." Newton's "considerable time" becomes permission for each of us to accept the slowness our own step-by-step journeys might take. [1]

Newton wrote a number of hymns that chronicled and celebrated his transformational journey. "Amazing Grace," written in the 1770s, is perhaps his best-known hymn. Later he wrote these words—words that describe the transformation not only of John Newton, but also of Lazarus, myself, and perhaps you as well:

> I am not what I ought to be.
> I am not what I want to be.
> I am not what I hope to be.
> But by the grace of God, I am not what I was. [2]

Newton's words speak of a past, present, and future movement in the transformational journey. His life bears witness to an important insight about how ordinary people experience the renovation of their lives. First, we emerge from the tomb, then we take steps—sometimes forward, sometimes wobbly, and sometimes even backward. But we're moving, and ultimately we're moving forward. It is not an instant, total transformation. It's a step-by-step journey of considerable time.

We observe another man's journey of makeover in the psalms of David. He began life as a shepherd boy and ended it as a celebrated king of Israel. His psalms reflect glorious victories in battle, and private, agonizing defeat in the battles against lust in his own heart. Sometimes his prayers exude excitement and awe. In others, we feel his discontent and frustration. In Psalm 23 he literally wants nothing and in Psalm 69 he desperately wants out of his emotional and spiritual black hole. We see his passionate worship in Psalm 8 and his lament over a God who seems distant in Psalm 10.

Like Newton, David gives us permission for a slow journey of transformation. In other words, he reminds us that while God longs to see us completely satisfied in Christ, He knows the sinfulness of our own hearts and the struggles of our circumstances. Even the children of Israel in the midst of their Exodus from Egypt walked a zigzagged path, often wanting to return to the life they knew—the life of the tomb, the life of onions and garlic. John's final book in the Bible, the Revelation, describes entire churches that have zigzagged their way through life and need a course correction. One of the New Testament churches has "lost their first love." Another church has "a reputation of being alive" but is dead (Rev. 3:1), while another church is merely "lukewarm." Individuals, families, churches, and even nations stumble on the way to Jesus.

Throughout our lives we see God offering us the choice to experience the life he has promised us, even after we repeatedly leave the path or fall down along the way. Thankfully we're not given just one chance to get it right. With this comfort in mind, we keep moving forward toward new life.

THE JOURNEY METAPHOR

The psalmist exclaims, "Blessed are those whose strength is in you, who have set their hearts on *pilgrimage*" (Ps. 84:5). From birth to the grave, we are on a pilgrimage—a journey toward our true home, our final destination. In fact the pilgrimage, or journey, metaphor is one of the best ways to describe the long, arduous path we walk, crawl, dance, grieve, and navigate on our way to transformation.[3] As Howard Baker, a professor at Denver Seminary, writes, "The biblical and classical image of 'journey' provides a robust metaphor to frame this life of following Jesus and to order our imaginations. It captures the attributes of movement, purpose, and destination that comprise the process of Christ being formed in us."[4]

Many authors through the ages sought to define this journey concept that is so pronounced in the Bible. Some have developed theories, others have defined stages, and still others have created outlines and diagramed steps complete with charts and maps! Their literary metaphors offer us images and language that help us describe our own progress.

St. Theresa of Avila developed what she called an "interior castle" with various rooms that defined levels and degrees of intimacy with God.

John Bunyan, imprisoned for twelve years with only his Bible to study, crafted one of the most beloved accounts of the Christian life in his spiritual classic, *Pilgrim's Progress*. Even the title hints at the *progress* of one pilgrim's spiritual journey. The main character, Christian, climbs the Hill Difficulty, travels through the Slough of Despond, and visits Vanity Fair.

In the twentieth century C. S. Lewis offered us the journey of four children through a magical, spiritual land in *The Chronicles of Narnia*. Their adventures through an ordinary wardrobe in an old English manor house led them to animals, witches, and a Christlike lion named Aslan.

Scholarly investigations of the spiritual life draw from psychology, religion, and medicine. For example, James A. Fowler's monumental work, *Stages of Faith: The Psychology of Human Development and the Quest for Meaning* combined and synthesized the theories of Erik Erikson, Jean Piaget, and Lawrence Kohlberg to describe a progressive development of one's faith journey. Fowler's theories have profoundly influenced educators, counselors, spiritual directors, and the clergy.

Churches of the liturgical tradition guide Christians through the calendar year in a progressive fashion because they see the calendar year as a journey of pilgrimage through seasons, events, and encounters.

However we refer to it, the spiritual life is a pilgrimage moving from one place to another. You can call it stages, phases, seasons, or degrees—but in the end, what is important to note is forward movement. Just as Jesus called, "Lazarus, come forth!" He calls us forward—not backward or sideways. This is not an ordinary journey.

It is a journey to become like Christ. We are traveling to the life Jesus promised.

FOLLOWING THE LIGHT OF JESUS

When I meet with a person or a couple for spiritual direction, often I will light a candle in the first few moments, reminding us of the reality that Jesus is the light. We pray and ask for the light of Jesus to give us direction. The candle is a small but important reminder that we need the light to dispel our darkness. When the light of Christ pushes back darkness, we move from sin to repentance, from brokenness to wholeness. We are transformed when we move toward light, not darkness.

In the light of our new life, eventually we see more, experience more, and taste the goodness of God more deeply. But it takes time for the eyes of our mind, heart, and soul to adjust to the light, the surroundings, and the group of stunned people staring at us as we stumble forward. In contrast to who was originally buried there, we emerge from the tomb as very different people. People might expect us—or even want us—to fall back to old habits. Even if we've been involved in a Christian community while hiding in the tomb, we can get lost in the maze of choices, programs, and leaders available to us. How will we know if we are headed in the right direction? How will we keep moving forward in our quest to be transformed people? What if people disapprove of our journey? What if we find ourselves back in the tomb and people give up on us emerging again? Or what if we miss the tomb and *want* to go back—to get away from the glare of new life?

In the midst of a recent spiritual direction session, I asked a man, "Why do you choose to remain in your tomb, when you know that freedom and life are outside?"

Almost embarrassed, he said, "At least in here, I know my life. I'm used to it. I don't know what's out there and what's waiting on me."

This man's response articulates many of the fears we have about taking steps away from the tomb. Our hollowed-out, cold tombs are safe because they are familiar to us. In the tomb we have learned to nurture wounds and not heal from them. Our pupils remain dilated because we grow accustomed to the darkness.

If we step into the light, we might become uncomfortable. We might have to quit doing something that we actually like, actually find ourselves longing for. The tomb gives us what we are used to. The tomb does not challenge us to change. In the light there's no telling what Jesus might ask us to do.

I know this because of my own experience emerging from the tomb. As crazy as it sounds, I actually like to work. I find it fascinating and fulfilling to help people experience the Lazarus life. But because of my own soul-sickness that I have described, a pull is within me not to take good care of myself. I begin to believe the lie that work will give me life. Work will satisfy me. I can spend hours in conversation and lose track of time. I can get lost in my world of words and writing.

My wife knows this about me all too well. Gwen tells me that when I'm working on a project she's often scared to knock on my door and ask if I'd like some coffee. She's afraid of my reaction to this interruption. In the past I must have reared up and communicated, through my tone of voice, "No! Don't speak to me about taking a break! I want to work.

I want to stay in my office and forget my life, forget you, and forget
other things." Of course, I don't say that with words. But the message is
implied. When I hear of Gwen's experience, I realize that my old habits
become a safe tomb for me. Even now my computer seems to call out to
me when I pass by it saying, "Come to me. Come sit with me and you
will find your life." For people with an addiction like mine, the pathway
back to the tomb can seem very appealing at times. What tomb allures
you?

I recently visited one of America's largest churches to meet with a
pastor who is in charge of the discipleship ministry. We spoke about
the culture in the office. Was it toxic? Was there a sense of community?
Was the office a safe place for people to grow in relationship with one
another as well as accomplish tasks and projects? I asked if the senior
pastor modeled a healthy lifestyle for the staff or was he a workaholic
(like me?).

The discipleship pastor told me a simple yet stunning practice that
the entire office practiced. Every day at 10 a.m. and 3 p.m., everyone—
and he meant everyone—took a mandatory break for fifteen minutes.
All staff had to be out of their offices, without their cells phones and
without their PDAs, and come to the courtyard just to talk. He told
me that once he had taken his cell phone on break and continued
an "urgent" conversation out in the courtyard until the senior pastor
tapped him on the shoulder and said, "Nothing is more important than
you taking a break right now."

That's a healthy working and "churching" environment! I wanted
to celebrate! I wanted to find that senior pastor and say, "Where were
you in my dark years?" But I also know that if I worked in such an

environment, I would probably resent mandatory breaks at times. It is more familiar and comfortable for me to take just one more phone call than it is to take a break.

Stumbling out of your dark tomb might be awkward and uncomfortable at first. But remember, each step forward is one step closer to the Voice of Love—one wobbly step at a time. Taking steps from darkness to light is not about destination. It's about movement, movement toward the Voice of Love that calls you out.

GOD-AWARENESS AND SELF-AWARENESS

My own forward movement involves examining the assumptions I hold about how life works. Just as Lazarus could not have moved forward if he didn't know where he was on the path to Jesus, I cannot move forward without exploring how my childhood, circumstances, and belief system affect me today.

I sometimes challenge a good friend of mine on some of her beliefs by asking, "How did you come up with your answer on this issue?" She inevitably tells me, "My daddy was a Baptist minister, and he always said ..." Her father must have downloaded hours of information into her head on many issues. But even Baptist ministers don't always know the truth on every subject. Believe me, I was one.

As we become more alert to our own condition, we become more aware of what lies we believe about God and ourselves. I mentioned earlier how important John Calvin's words about self-knowledge were to me in my own life. Knowing God and knowing ourselves are twin journeys that we all must take to experience spiritual transformation. As we become more God-aware, we become more self-aware. The reverse is also true.

The Jewish prophet Isaiah teaches us a valuable lesson about the connection between self-awareness and God-awareness. In Isaiah 6, Isaiah describes a vision through which he became more aware of God. This awakening led to his becoming aware of his own condition: "'Woe to me!' I cried. 'I am ruined! For I am a man of unclean lips, and I live among a people of unclean lips, and my eyes have seen the King, the Lord Almighty'" (Isa. 6:5). As Isaiah became more aware of God's purity, he became more aware of his own impurity. Awareness of God led to awareness of himself, which led to speaking God's truth to others.

God-Awareness

Many of the artists who painted Lazarus leaving the tomb show Lazarus's eyes riveted on Jesus—not on the people who are covering their noses because of the smell, not on the tomb door that had just been removed, but simply on Jesus. If you'll take a look at Giotto's rendering, you can see this focus. Only Jesus' voice could have transported Lazarus from death's grip back to life. So Jesus, and only Jesus, was the object of Lazarus's attention.

As God reveals His heart of love to us through calling us out of the tomb, we find ourselves becoming more and more aware of His voice, His ways, His nature, and His desires. Yet busyness, obligations, commitments, and chores can distract us from awareness of God.

One of the ways to practice our God-awareness is through spiritual exercises, what some people call "spiritual disciplines." The word discipline means "making space." We make space for God by deliberately spending time with Him. Spiritual disciplines, or exercises, help the soul the way physical exercises help the body. Through them we begin to use spiritual muscles that have atrophied in the tomb. Since transformation does not happen by amassing more information about Jesus, we need to grow in life-giving ways so that our awareness of God can deepen and we find ourselves enjoying His presence more and more.

Self-Awareness

Focusing on God includes focusing on who He created us to be. A knowledge of God without a knowledge of self leads to the dangerous religion that the Pharisees practiced. Jesus challenged this group because they refused to look inward—to look inside their own lives for the darkness where sinful motives, pride, and unhealthy desires lie.[5] Jesus told the Pharisees to "scour" the inside and not just polish the outside. It is the "inside" world where we need transformation the most. Private habits, secret addictions, bitterness, anger, pride, and a host of other issues trip us up.

Self-awareness means accepting the fact that we do not walk perfectly on the path in front of us. We do not become resigned to those weaknesses, but we also do not deny their presence. Psychologist and author David Benner reminds us, "Even things about yourself that you most deeply want to change must first be accepted—even embraced.... Until we are willing to accept the unpleasant truths of our existence, we rationalize or deny responsibility for our behavior."[6]

The Danish theologian Søren Kirkeegaard wrote a prayer that I often voice to God: "And now Lord, with your help, I shall become myself." We become our true selves as we accept ourselves just as we know God accepts us. We accept our condition, our graveclothes, and our weaknesses as well as our strengths. Only then can we move forward to be transformed into the people God calls us to be.

Do you like where your life is headed right now? What baggage of past addictions, disappointments, and assumptions are you carrying along the way? What does moving toward Jesus look like to you today? We each need to find our own steps of freedom as we emerge from the tomb, always remembering that self-knowledge and God-knowledge grow together.

KEEP COMING FORWARD

After my time in the monastery, I arrived home ready to experience transformation as a pastor, leader, father, and husband—but after a period of time, I felt lost once more. The pressure of my work began to creep in, and old patterns began to emerge. I was trying to live the life I wanted—the life Jesus was calling me to live—but I was stuck.

A wise and trusted friend came to visit me one day and listened to me lament about my confusion as to how I should focus my life. She leaned back in her chair and simply said, "Steve, keep coming forward." I recognized her words deep in my soul as truth. These words acknowledged my sense of struggle, my sense of desire for freedom, and my longing for real life. These were the words Jesus spoke to Lazarus. Keep coming forward! The only way to experience the life I wanted so deeply was to keep coming forward.

You may be disappointed with your progress and your journey, but sometimes, doing the right thing is simply the right thing to do and this starts with taking one more step in the right direction. The next plateau may be the one where you can see how far you've come when you look back. The next bend on the trail might reveal the perspective you've been waiting for all along.

In my own life I soon realized that I could not go back. Nothing in the tomb was "for" me. Only Jesus was for me. Jesus had given me what I wanted and needed, and my soul-sickness only improved by moving toward Him.

I imagine that Lazarus must have felt something similar when he heard Jesus call to him. He heard his name. He heard his friend's voice. He got up and started moving. He knew nothing was left in the tomb for him. The tomb was death and Jesus was life. It was a simple choice: Should I go back? What is back there for me?

What if Lazarus had said, "Oh, Jesus, I'm not ready to come out yet," or "Jesus, it's great to be alive but couldn't you have done something about these graveclothes?" What if he said, "This wasn't what I was expecting"? Being alive was enough for Lazarus. He moved toward Jesus.

Lazarus's emergence from the tomb reminds us that God invites us to participate with him in our own transformation. Paul reminds us to "put off your old self" and to "put on the new self" (Eph. 4:22–23). We are not automatically dressed up in new clothes or new ways when we start to follow Jesus. The ongoing process of "putting on" is clearly our responsibility. Paul explores this idea further for us in his letter to the Colossians: "So, chosen by God for this new life of love, dress in the wardrobe of God picked out for you." He then goes on to state the wardrobe we are to wear: compassion, kindness, humility, quiet strength, discipline, forgiveness—"and regardless of what else you put on wear love. It's your basic all-purpose garment. Never be without it" (Col. 3:12–14 MSG).

Paul reminds us elsewhere:

> What I'm getting at, friends, is that you should simply keep on doing what you've done from the beginning. When I was living among you, you lived in responsive obedience. Now that I'm separated from you, keep it up. Better yet, redouble your efforts. Be energetic in your life of salvation, reverent and sensitive before God. That energy is God's energy, an energy deep within you, God himself willing and working at what will give him the most pleasure. (Phil. 2:12–13 MSG)

Did you catch Paul's words here? We are to: "keep on doing," "show responsive obedience," "redouble your efforts," "be energetic," "be reverent," "be sensitive before God."

But notice that the energy to do this is God's energy at work deep within us. *Transformation happens when God's energy and our efforts converge.* We see this paradox in Lazarus's life. The power of God and the forward movement of Lazarus converged into a transformed life.

Walking toward Jesus involves many acts of surrendering our will, our longings, and our desires. God may grant us our desires a hundredfold, just as He did for Mary and Martha. But even Jesus had to surrender His will to God in Gethsemane when He said, "Not my will but yours." If we hold on to *our* way, we'll soon find that we will not be in the way that leads to a transformed life.

When I was encouraged to read the red-letter words of Jesus and stay focused on His teaching and study His ways of doing life, I experienced a great "aha" moment. Before that time the ways of powerful, successful people intrigued me more than the way of Jesus. I had to come back to this very important lesson: If Jesus said He was the resurrection and life, then I should be about the business of focusing on Him. That insight alone has helped me make tremendous progress in being a transformed person.[7]

As John tells us, "Whoever claims to live in him must walk as Jesus did" (1 John 2:6). The journey toward being transformed men and women is the way of Jesus. No matter how much we stumble on the journey, His way becomes the way to new life. So let us consider the way and let us walk in it.

COMPLETELY NEW

Thomas Merton, a Catholic monk and spiritual writer in the twentieth century, was once asked, "What do your vows oblige you to do?" Merton replied, "My [vows] are a commitment to a total inner transformation of one sort or another; a commitment to become a completely new man."[8]

The journey that you and I are on is a journey to become a completely new person, a journey in which the Christ in us gains more and more space. A journey in which He is increasing and we are decreasing.[9] Yet an inner transformation of "one sort or another" happens in steps, stages, and seasons.

As we have seen, our movement forward in the spiritual life is messy and awkward, but it is still *movement*. Would you want the same marriage you had when you were first married? Do you want your relationships with your friends to stay at the same level as the day you met? Do you want to have the same expertise in your job today as you did your first day of work? For most of us, the answer is "No!" We want to grow. We want to change. We yearn for transformation. We long to move our legs and arms and open our squinting eyes and get out of that tomb. This step-by-step movement is a step forward. It is a step toward the life we want, the life only Jesus can give.

NOTES

[1] For a more in-depth study of John Newton's conversion story and the "anatomy of conversion," see Gerald L. Sittser's *Water from a Deep Well* (Downers Grove, IL: IVP, 2008), 232–255.

[2] John Newton would customarily offer a blessing before the evening meal. In one of these blessings, Newton is recorded as giving a longer version of this quote, which is found in the "Westminster Shorter Catechism Project" by John Whitecross. http://www.bpc.org/resources/whitecross/wsc_wh_035.html accessed June 10, 2007.

[3] Alister McGrath's *The Journey* is an excellent resource to understand the journey of the Christian life.

[4] Howard Baker, "The Spiritual Journey," in *The Transformation of a Man's Heart*, edited by Stephen W. Smith (Downers Grove, IL: IVP, 2006), 25.

[5] See Matthew 23:25.

6 David G. Benner, *The Gift of Being Yourself* (Downers Grove, IL: IVP, 2004), 56–57.

7 Eugene Peterson has given us a gift in his inspiring book, *The Jesus Way* (Eerdmans, 2007). I highly recommend this book to help you explore the way Jesus did His life and His example for us today.

8 As quoted in *Alive in Christ* by Maxie Dunnam (Nashville: Upper Room, 1986), 51

9 These are the words of John the Baptist about his cousin Jesus, when John was stating his role and position related to Jesus Christ in John 3:30.

Chapter Seven

NAMING THE GRAVECLOTHES:
RECOGNIZING THE THINGS THAT BIND YOU

*The dead man came out, his hands
and feet wrapped with strips of linen,
and a cloth around his face.*

—John 11:44

- When we emerge from the tomb, we still wear the outer reality
  of what is left to be transformed.
- Naming what is holding us back from Jesus will help us take
  steps toward Him.
- Many Christians struggle with self-rejection, fear, guilt, blame
  and shame, and disappointment. Only God can help us lighten
  the load of those graveclothes.

Take a moment and look at Giotto's rendering of Lazarus again. Lazarus stands at the door of the tomb, his gray face set like flint in the direction of Jesus. His body is mummified. Jesus is but a few feet away and Lazarus is out of the tomb, but Lazarus seems unable to move. His graveclothes hold him back. And in contrast to the colorful garments of Jesus, Mary, and Martha and all the bystanders, Lazarus's muslin graveclothes are bleak, colorless, and austere. Could Giotto have been trying to tell us that resurrection might look different than what we think? Lazarus emerged from the tomb a new person, yet showing signs of what he looked like when he went in. He didn't come out of the tomb dressed in vivid blues, warm golds, and hues of red. In Giotto's painting, it's obvious that Lazarus is going to move forward. But first he needs freedom from what binds him.[1]

As we've seen in the previous chapter, graveclothes can cause us to stumble as we emerge from the tomb. Yes, we are alive—but barely. We hear the Voice of Love calling us forward, onward, and outward, but we can't move. Is the mummified, gray life of graveclothes the life we want to live?

THE FABRIC OF OUR GRAVECLOTHES

Like an iceberg, which reveals only one tenth of its existence above the water line, a whole lot more lies underneath—nine tenths in fact—that can wreak havoc and cause major damage. It's the same way with graveclothes. To be free of them, we have to look more closely at them to find the end of one and the beginning of another. All the graveclothes wound together make a mummified body that isn't "running, leaping, and dancing for joy" as other recipients of their own miracles do elsewhere in the Bible. When we unwrap each one individually we experience new life—new possibilities—freedom and yes, transformation!

The author Frederick Buechner writes of the power of sin being "centrifugal." Sin presses out to the periphery of our lives, affecting everything and everyone around us. What's within us can come out like a gravecloth—eventually tangling us up in its vice and grip. Many of us believe that through information and education, we can maneuver away from sin's influence. Some may try to "manage" their sin as Dallas Willard says. But sin is more wild than rational. It wields a power that overwhelms and enslaves us like tightly wound graveclothes. Trapped by darkened desires, we feel the tug-of-war in our hearts. Sin is in the fabric of our graveclothes. We've all sinned and fallen short of God's glory. This conniving and deceitful and interestingly woven fabric becomes an unending source of struggle and strife for us. This side of heaven we will always have to deal with the texture, weaving ability, and wrapping power it has on us, in us, and around us. We simply cannot escape sin's grip and its ability to trip us up in the journey called life.

The apostle Paul lamented this struggle in Romans 7:21–24 (MSG):

> It happens so regularly that it's predictable. The moment I decide to do well, sin is there to trip me up. I truly delight in God's commands, but it's pretty obvious that not all of me joins in that delight. Parts of me covertly rebel, and just when I least expect it, they take charge. I've tried everything and nothing helps. I'm at the end of my rope.

Hebrews 12:1 (NLT) says, "Let us strip off every weight that slows us down, especially the sin that so easily trips us up. And let us run with endurance the race that God has set before us." Another Bible translation gives more insight to this verse: "It means we'd better get on with it. Strip down, start running—and never quit! No extra spiritual fat, no parasitic sins" (MSG). It's almost as if the writer of Hebrews was thinking of Lazarus's graveclothes when this was written. The graveclothes of "parasitic sins" have to be "stripped down" so we can begin to run to Jesus to gain the life he has promised.

I am finding it helpful to look at the graveclothes as things that are actually preventing me from what I desire most: freedom, life, and transformation. Each gravecloth can become a symbol of something that is inhibiting our movement forward, restricting us from experiencing the life that Jesus promises and robbing us of the possibilities of transformation. The graveclothes can become a part of the consequences of sin in our lives and lingering reminders of the nicks, bruises, and wounds we have suffered in life. Like Lazarus, we must be free of them if we want to experience transformation.

To be free of them, we must name them and know them as foes that hinder us on the journey forward.

THE POWER OF NAMING

After God created the heavens, earth, water, sky, and people, and creatures to populate the earth, He gave a significant instruction to Adam. He told Adam to *name* the animals (Gen. 2:19). By naming the creatures roaming the fresh earth, the first man formed a method of communication and recognition for himself and all humanity. He also showed his domination over the creatures of the world.

We use names today, of course, to identify everything from pets to illnesses. How many times have you heard a toddler ask: "What's that?" From the time we are young, we want to understand our surroundings. *Naming* gives us an ability to understand, associate, and relate to our world around us.

Anyone who has spent time in a foreign country without knowing the language knows that not being able to identify places, people, and objects by name makes one feel incompetent and frustrated. Once we have words to put to our surroundings, we are not as intimidated. The same is true for our thoughts and emotions. If our past relationship with a sibling, for instance, is a vague collection of angry and painful memories, those memories will always have domination over us. If we are able to name those feelings ("I feel like you always have to be better than me" or "I feel hurt that you never take the initiative to come visit"), we are able to address their root and be in better control of them. Naming helps us understand. Naming helps us overcome. Naming the issue that is really bothering us helps us communicate.

A striking example of this is recorded in Mark 5 when Jesus confronts a nameless, tormented man along the road, in the region of the Gerasenes. This possessed man needed deliverance from an evil spirit; many spirits, in fact. His hands and feet had been chained, but he broke them and lived in the tombs. Night and day he cried and cut himself with stones.

When Jesus encountered the man, He commanded, "Come out of this man, you evil spirit!" The man of the tombs addressed Jesus by one of His names: "What do you want, Jesus, Son of the Most High God? Swear to God that you won't torture me!" To this Jesus countered, "What is *your* name?" The possessed man answered, "Legion," revealing that many demons were tormenting the man (Mark 5:7–8).[2] Jesus then cast out the demons.

Identifying the demons' name and nature reduced their grip on the man. They were no longer mysterious, all-powerful beings; they were demons Jesus could address by name and dominate. As the demons were named, Jesus brought about transformation. Only when the false names were cast out could the man from the tombs embrace his true name: the beloved.

Until we identify the *legion* of attitudinal and emotional graveclothes wrapped around us, they will constrict our hearts and prevent us from moving freely toward life. Knowing what has bound us up will help to free us.

FIVE COMMON GRAVECLOTHES

When I met Peter a few years ago, he was tentatively emerging from his tomb. Peter became a Christian in college where he majored in business. While his conversion to Christianity changed him, Peter nursed a deep, secret obsession with gambling. Two years into his marriage, Peter's wife discovered this devastating secret. The graveclothes he had worn for years were finally identified. The weight of those clothes, the energy to hide them, the passion to maintain them, and the guilt over their existence sapped his inner life. But now he's asking for help, courageously naming his sins and moving toward Jesus.

The God who knows us by name recognizes that each of us has unique issues that need attention. Jesus used Peter's unbridled brashness, Thomas's wavering doubt, Mary's misplaced passion, and Martha's secret obsessions in their individual transformation processes. Knowing our weaknesses as well as our strengths provides valuable insight into how God may want to work in a specific area of our lives to bring freedom.

I want to explore five of the most common graveclothes that I encounter today in the spiritual life: self-rejection, fear, guilt, shame and blame, and disappointment. If I presume to understand these graveclothes, it is because I struggle with them too. Kierkegaard defined sin as "the steadfast refusal to be your one true self." We are the beloved of Christ, that is our "one true self," and these graveclothes keep us from moving toward being the beloved. As we are learning, graveclothes are constricting and covering, they blind us and bind us in our efforts to really live a transformed life.

As we name the things that bind us, keep in mind that we might wear a few or many graveclothes. Sometimes we can't tell where one gravecloth ends and the next one begins. Take a look at Giotto's painting and you'll see what I mean. But with thought, reflection, and prayer, we can identify what is holding us back and begin to unravel the grip of the graveclothes and move toward Jesus—the source of life.

Self-Rejection

In a spiritual direction session Julie confessed to Gwen and me, "I hate myself." When we asked her to elaborate, she recited what seemed like a rehearsed list. She began with what she didn't like about her body: She was "too short, too fat, and too average" to attract a man. Then she described how she felt useless at work and insecure in her friendships.

After a few minutes of listening, Gwen asked, "Julie, why do you think God loves you?" The question halted Julie's tirade of self-hatred. As we talked more, we began to identify the untruths that held her captive. Julie's sense of being the *Beloved* of God had been eroded by choosing to believe lies about herself. These lies found their way into Julie's heart, causing a gravecloth of self-rejection to constrict her heart and her spiritual vitality. She felt unworthy to live and be free.

Over time Julie began to listen for the Voice of Love rather than her own voice of self-hatred. She had to do soul work on the root of her feelings of inferiority, but through prayer and the encouragement of friends, she gained insight about her true identity. Julie now looks like a new person. Her smile is real. Her eyes are full of light and she carries herself with confidence.

When we begin to unwrap the dreadful gravecloth of self-rejection, we'll feel the tension between accepting ourselves as God accepts us and the negative feelings we harbor about ourselves. Until we discover and accept our true identity as the beloved—the one in whom God is truly delighted—we can never be completely free from the grip of self-doubt, defeat, and inner confusion.[3]

As we explored in chapter 4, when Jesus calls us, He calls us with a Voice of Love. By naming the gravecloth of self-rejection, we can loosen its grip and move toward that voice. We silence the jeering and say *yes* to the Jesus who says, "I have loved you with an everlasting love; I have drawn you with loving-kindness.... You are mine" (Jer. 31:3 and Isa. 43:1).

Self-rejection often becomes one of the greatest enemies of the spiritual life. This dangerous gravecloth can cause a man to feel inadequate and a woman to feel insecure in her true identity. It robs us of the joy of living as the beloved!

Fear

James, a middle-aged sales manager, attended one of our retreats a few years ago. He told us during our first evening together, "What I have feared the most has finally happened. I got fired today." His private fear went beyond concerns about losing his income. His fear had taken up residence in his heart and became tied to his very identity.

When I spoke about taking off graveclothes on that cool Colorado night, James said, "There's no doubt about it. I have been gripped by fear and I need to get rid of it." As we talked further, it became clear that James's sense of self-worth was anchored in his job. His confusion with soul and role had eroded his sense of value, with or without a job. Since his sales were slow and he wasn't meeting the quota assigned him, he spiraled. Now, without a job, James is unraveling a gravecloth that gripped him for years. Who is James, really? "Just" a salesman, or someone else? Who are you?

James is not alone. Fear seems to hide itself as a gravecloth at first. You might quickly read through this and say, "Not me. I don't have a problem with fear." But let's look closer.

When we feel safe enough to admit what is on our hearts, we face a long buffet line of fears.

- *Health*—What if I get sick? What if I'm disabled? Who will take care of me? Will there be a cure? Many of us fear losing our independence and well-being.

- *Relationships*—Does anybody really love me? Will I ever get married? What if she leaves me? What if he has an affair? The fear of being alone seems epidemic today.

- *Money*—Do I have enough to make it? What if I don't? How can I keep up with everyone else? We fear not being secure financially or able to provide for our families.

- *Spirituality*—Is God really there? Does He care? Am I by myself? Will He answer my prayers? The fear of facing life without God makes all of life seem shaky.

- *Wounds*—Do I have to limp through life with this wound in my soul? Is there any real hope for transformation? The fear of living with the same pain, shame, or addiction forever can be debilitating.

- *Work*—Can I do this job? Do I matter enough to even get a job? How much do I have to endure in a difficult job? We fear living with regret about our vocational choices or never finding a vocation that fulfills us.

Fear finds a way to rob us of life in subtle as well as bold ways. You may not have a dramatic phobia, but a deep-seated fear might constrict your heart in ways you don't even realize.

When we tug at a gravecloth like fear, we can't settle for a quick fix. After naming the fear—something we might feel is a scary step in itself—we must look underneath the surface for the reasons it riddles

our souls. Some of these reasons can be "smelly" because they have rot-
ted inside us for years.

For example, I counseled a woman named Becca who fears close
relationships. I asked her why, and at first she said, "No one has time to
get to know other people anymore." But later conversations revealed a
deeper pain. Becca's mother was very ill as Becca was growing up and
was often in the hospital. Years later Becca's older brother was killed in
Vietnam. In college one of her closest friends betrayed her and cut off
their relationship. After that Becca decided not to get close to anyone.
Fear had wrapped around her heart, her friendships, and her desire for
community. When she examined this moldy gravecloth, she began to
wrest herself from the past and experience a freedom in relationships she
had not known before.

If we believe that God is unwilling or unable to speak to us personally, then we will remain trapped in the tomb of fear. This is not what
Jesus described when he spoke of the abundant life (John 10:10), rivers of
life flowing inside of us (John 7:38), and intimacy with the Father (John
17:11). Fear drains the reservoir of living water from our hearts and souls.

Paul's closing words to the young Timothy offer consolation when
we're afraid. Paul was in a horrid prison. Timothy had lost him as a
close mentor. It looked like the end. Paul knew his own outcome and
was trying to prepare his younger friend for what was about to happen. In the darkness of a tomb-like prison, the apostle wrote these
words: "For God did not give us a spirit of timidity (of cowardice, of
craven and cringing and fawning fear), but [He has given us a spirit]
of power and of love and of a calm and well-balanced mind and discipline and self-control" (2 Tim 1:7 AB).

Paul had reason to fear, knowing that he would soon be executed. But in the suffocating darkness, he held forth the candle of truth. Fear does not emanate from God. It comes from a trembling heart, a shaking soul. Fear is birthed in darkened tombs where we imagine the worst. It is then nourished in secrets, lies, and half-truths. Perhaps when Paul wrote to Timothy, he was thinking of the psalmist's words: "Powerful people harass me without cause, but my heart trembles only at your word" (Ps. 119:161 NLT).

The Voice of Love calling us from the tomb is more powerful than the voice of fear taunting us to stay put. It reminds us that we belong to God, not fear (see Rom. 8:37–39). We were not created to live in the tomb. We were made to be alive in Christ.

Guilt

The first time I met with Dale, I asked him why he'd scheduled a session with me. He paused, reached back into his past life, and explained, "I need to be forgiven of what happened twenty-one years ago. I got a girl pregnant, and out of fear, she got an abortion. I've worn that guilt as a heavy cloak for twenty-one years. It's robbed me of peace and contentment. I need help." Our conversations began a journey of exploring Dale's feelings of guilt, isolation, loneliness, and remorse. Sin and guilt walk hand in hand. Once we've sinned, we can wear the gravecloth of guilt for years, even for a lifetime.

Carol came to our retreat where we were leading a group in practicing the spiritual disciplines of silence and solitude. She struggled with this spiritual discipline because it made her feel guilty about wasting time. She said, "Shouldn't I be reading a book or journaling or *doing* something?" As Carol examined how Jesus regularly practiced solitude, she began to relax. This realization helped free her from false guilt about not "doing enough for God."

Guilt, more than any other gravecloth, is a heavy load to drag through churches, small groups, marriages, friendships, and on the job. Fredrick Buechner explains it this way:

> The danger of guilt, both personal and collective, is less that we won't take it to heart than that we'll take it to heart overmuch and let it fester there in ways that we ourselves often fail to recognize.... It is about as hard to absolve yourself of your own guilt as it is to sit in your own lap.[4]

Feeling culpable for a wrongdoing is something God uses to call us back into fellowship and intimacy. After King David's adulterous tryst with Bathsheba, he lamented, "My guilt has overwhelmed me like a burden too heavy to bear (Ps. 38:4). In an earlier psalm David also wrote of his struggle with guilt: "When I kept silent my bones wasted away through my groaning all day long.... Then I acknowledged my sin to you and did not cover up my inequity. I said, 'I will confess my transgressions to the Lord—and you forgave the guilt of my sin'" (Ps. 32:3–5). David describes a healthy guilt that is not a gravecloth but a tool of the Holy Spirit. C. S. Lewis said that God uses true guilt as an "inner alarm system" that reveals the error of our ways. But not all guilt is healthy and not all guilt points to sin.

When other people judge, criticize, and condemn us, we can

plunge into cesspools of false guilt. Swiss psychologist Paul Tournier said false guilt "comes as result of judgments and suggestions of men." A twenty-one-year-old college student described his struggle with false guilt this way: "My dad acts like judge, jury, and executioner when I do something wrong. He makes me feel utterly worthless." False guilt causes us to sink in defeat rather than rise up and move out of the tomb.

When we succumb to false guilt, we believe we should have or could have done something more—something different. A nagging sense that we should have done this or that in life, work, and marriage robs us of our life and freedom. A man came up to me at a retreat a few years ago after I finished speaking about the gravecloth of guilt. He shared that his son had died tragically in a hunting accident five years earlier. The father felt responsible. He said, "Why couldn't I have done something? Why didn't I take the bullet?" As we talked through the tragedy, it became apparent that this man was bound by guilt. As we prayed together, we asked God to unwrap his heart of guilt and give him the peace promised to us in Scripture. We asked for a peace that goes beyond a human's ability to comprehend: the "surpassing" or "transcending peace" described in Philippians 4:7. Later the man shared that he felt as if a heavy burden had been lifted from his shoulders. No doubt he'll need to continue unwrapping the gravecloth of guilt until he's at peace about his son, but one layer of guilt had been removed.

God uses guilt so we feel uneasy about our wrongdoings. But wrongdoing is different from "wrong being." Wrong being is feeling condemned by our own hearts or by the voice of others. Wrong being results in a sense of worthlessness that undermines God's forgiveness and our ability to trust that if God accepts us, then surely we can accept ourselves. Feelings of worthlessness are a signal that we still have graveclothes to unwrap.

The truth of Scripture loosens the grip of guilt's gravecloth and silences its ugly, nagging voice. Consider Paul's words in Romans 8:1–2 (MSG):

> With the arrival of Jesus, the Messiah, that fateful dilemma is resolved. Those who enter into Christ's being-here-for-us no longer have to live under a continuous, low-lying black cloud. A new power is in operation. The Spirit of life in Christ, like a strong wind, has magnificently cleared the air, freeing you from a fated lifetime of brutal tyranny at the hands of sin and death.

Jesus holds the new power to rid ourselves of the gravecloth of guilt and put on the free-flowing clothes of a son or daughter of God.[5]

Shame and Blame

Shame and blame become toxic and twisted graveclothes for us to unravel because their work is often hidden—suppressed way below the surface of a person's outer body where the naked eye cannot see. Often something has happened in a person's past that is unresolved in the present and the graveclothes of shame and blame attempt to cover the wound and hinder the heart from beating with life and vigor. Shame and blame create a systemic infection that goes wild and rampant in the mind and heart of the one who wears these very smelly graveclothes. The graveclothes of shame and blame can be woven from feelings of inadequacy, wrong behavior, believing lies about our true identity as God's beloved sons and daughters, and a number of other sources. Each source of the root of shame and blame needs to be cleansed from the infection that pollutes the heart and disturbs the mind as we journey forward toward Jesus.

Betsy began unknowingly to wear shame and blame as graveclothes when she was molested and abused as a child. Those experiences made Betsy to feel as if she was trash and worthless. She wore those grave-clothes on her wedding night when she confessed to her new husband her fear of sexual intimacy. Bill is another example of how one begins to wear the graveclothes of shame and blame. Bill began to wear these graveclothes when he divorced his wife—the unthinkable sin in his long lineage of Christian ancestors—none of whom had ever been divorced. It was unthinkable—at least that was what he was led to believe about his heritage. Bill would be the first to publicly fail at marriage. His graveclothes would now be worn, making him feel less than anyone else in his family of Christian heritage.

The graveclothes of shame and blame are woven around our hearts when something from our past haunts us in the present that doesn't feel clean—feel right—or feel "Christian." When one wears these grave-clothes, feelings of being "less than anyone else," "too wounded to count," or similar feelings of inadequacy, we internally sabotage our true identity of being the beloved. We become something less than who we really are.

Jerry was born into a racist family. He was taught to hate people from other races. For years Jerry participated in meetings that bred hatred and disdained acceptance of people with different color skin. Jerry became a Christian a few years ago and now feels embarrassed by his participation and endorsement of hate groups. But it *was in his past*. How can Jerry work through the shame and blame he feels now that he's a Christian? It's an important question that we need to explore because there are many Jerrys in the world who struggle with something in their past that they long to be freed from.

Mary, a beautiful young woman, wore a Promise Ring—a ring signifying sexual purity—for years throughout high school and college. Her parents had given it to her on her 13th birthday. She intended "to save herself" until her wedding night for her husband. She shared with me that she feels "all bound up" with shame because she wasn't able to keep her promise. She met a young man in college who was in her campus ministry group. Love bred passion, and Mary lost her virginity. Her shame became an encircling snare that seemed to rob her of joy and freedom.

Jerry's and Mary's own graveclothes may not be that unique when we begin to look under the surface of our own graveclothes. Many of us may find things underneath that we are never proud of or embarrassed by. It seems like an endless list of possibilities, but some of the graveclothes that begin to bind the heart and constrict our lives can include: prejudice, jealousy, poverty, monetary success, lack of education or vocational credentials, physical attributes that we try to hide and cover up, religious heritages such as ultrafundamentalist beliefs and practices, or participation in spurious groups or cults that may have grabbed our minds as well as our hearts.

Blame and shame are twins that whisper into our hearts about repeated mistakes, incidents in our history, and failed attempts to change. They keep us stuck in the past. Blame says, "I've *done* wrong." Shame says, "I *am* wrong." When we live with shame and blame as graveclothes, we feel disqualified before we even begin the journey to Jesus. With our feet bound by blame and our heart bound by shame, we stagger but we don't really live. Repeated efforts to change that have failed seem to complicate the gravecloth issue because now we have to deal with the shame of never being able to break the cycle and feelings of being trapped.

The humorist Mark Twain pointedly said, "Man is the only animal that blushes or needs to." I've often felt the blush of blame and shame. Blame taunts me when I make a mistake. For example, when I yell at one of my sons rather than respond appropriately to him, blame says, "Steve, he's going to hate you because of what you have done. You made matters so much worse." Shame contributes by saying, "Steve you are a bad father. You will never get it right!"

Afraid to show their faces, blame and shame can resort to sending arrows deep into our hearts. Some of these messages hit emotional veins that bleed for years. We feel irrecoverable. But we can take deliberate actions to silence the chatter of blame and shame:

- We remind ourselves daily of our true identity by reading core Scriptures that tell the truth about who we are. We are God's beloved—no matter what![6]
- We remind ourselves that God's love is utterly unconditional. Love is not based on our ability to be loved. God's love is based on the fact that God chooses to love us.
- We use our own voice to quiet the hecklers. Developing our own voice means we gain the authority and confidence to call

blame and shame liars and deceivers. As we gain confidence, we find healing and grace to stand up to their sabotage.

- The toxic waste of blame and shame requires cleaning up. A part of working out our salvation (Phil. 2:12) means ridding ourselves of the pollution that has invaded our hearts. Learning to listen to the Voice of Love, practicing spiritual disciplines, and being spoken "into" by people who love us helps.

- A healthy Christian community hears the truth, practices love, and offers acceptance. Biblical community offered in Jesus' name can unwrap the graveclothes that grip us. Just as Jesus was "full of grace and truth" (John 1:14), spiritual communities can be too.

- Working through a specific gravecloth with a spiritual guide, mentor, or pastor can help bring resolution and offer hope. My own graveclothes have needed loving and trusted hands of friends much wiser than me to help me see how to begin the unraveling process. This process has helped me to realize the graveclothes that I can own and do something about and others that I need to lay at the feet of Jesus and ask for divine help!

It's crucial to call blame and shame by their names so we can understand their purpose and methods. Their ugly voices drown out the Voice of Love calling us forward, making us feel inadequate, helpless, weak, insecure, inferior, unworthy, and intimated.

Disappointment
I sometimes wonder if Lazarus had to give up any lingering feelings

of disappointment in his friend Jesus for not showing up in time. Resentment, anger, bitterness, and disappointment can entangle us in our movement forward. What if Lazarus stayed just outside the tomb having a pity party, relishing his wounds, and nursing resentment against God? One of the ways we lighten our load on the way to Jesus is by giving up an unforgiving heart toward those who have hurt or disappointed us, including God.

In chapter 2, we looked at how our expectations of God and others affect us. If we experience disappointment with God, or if someone else has let us down through an oversight or blatant offense, our disillusionment can hinder our forward movement toward Jesus. We can cling so tightly to our rights of being the "disappointed one" or "hurt one" that our expectations become a heavy load.

Several years ago a dear friend betrayed me. I felt I had been dealt a mortal blow. I nursed my wound thinking that I was entitled to be offended. But my unforgiving heart had to be set free from holding on to being the offended one. When I became aware of this, my anger soothed toward my friend. I was able to see that he wanted to reconcile with me and eventually was able to work on freeing myself from this particular gravecloth. Removing this gravecloth has required the help of wise friends and trusted men and women who have helped me unwrap layers of hurt feelings and built-up infection in my own heart from the disappointment, hurt, and devastation from a broken friendship. It's taken time, love, and skill for me to experience freedom and letting the hurt really go. Because the hurt was so deep, the removal of this gravecloth has been more of a process than an instant fix.

When we acknowledge how disappointed we are at times with God, others, and ourselves, we are free to explore our expectations and get to the source of our pain.

LIGHTENING THE LOAD

Authentic transformation is always messier than we expect it to be. Sometimes a gentle pull on one gravecloth causes everything to unravel. You think you'll never find the end and you may need many hands to free you. You might even feel you are wasting time. But consider the ways you will be better able to love yourself, God, and others when you are free from what binds you.

It might help to consider the apostle Paul's transformational journey. As a leader of the Pharisees, Paul was responsible for the death, killing, and persecution of the first followers of Jesus Christ. It was his duty to wipe the world clean of what he thought was a spurious infection in the Jewish faith.

After his conversion to Christianity on the road to Damascus, Paul went into the desert of Arabia for three years (see Gal. 1:17–18). That's right, three years of desert living! In the desert Paul took his own step-by-step journey into being a transformed man. There he intentionally worked through his own issues, regrets, and perhaps shame over what he had done. Silence became the balm to heal his heart, prayer became a refuge of strength, and much of the letters he eventually wrote to the New Testament church began to incubate in his heart and soul.

Was this a waste of time? Was anything getting "done"? Without taking the time to name his graveclothes, Paul would not have had the powerful influence he had in later years. Paul did the work of strengthening his heart, bolstering his faith, and growing in his intimacy with Jesus before beginning his official ministry. He was not perfect when he emerged from the desert, but he was free from many of the graveclothes that once bound him.

The possibilities for the names of graveclothes seem almost endless. Perhaps my suggestions have helped you to think of other ones that are specific to you or someone you know. But take heart—the Voice of Love is more powerful than anything that binds you. As you examine these clothes, be open to the Voice of Love calling you closer—calling you to rid yourself of spiritual restrictions and put on the beautifully colored clothes of grace.

NOTES

[1] See Matthew 26:12; Luke 23:56; John 19:39; and Acts 9:37.

[2] *Mark, New Bible Commentary*, eds, Guthrie, Motyer, Stibbs, Wiseman (Grand Rapids, MI: Wm. B. Eerdmans, Copyright 1970 Inter Varsity Press), 862.

[3] For more examination of the theme of being and becoming the beloved, see *Embracing Soul Care* by Stephen W. Smith (Kregel, 2006), pp. 47–60.

[4] Frederick Buechner, *Wishful Thinking: A Seeker's ABC* (San Francisco: HarperSanFrancisco, 1993), 39.

[5] See Psalm 103:10, 12; Isaiah 43:25; Isaiah 55:7.

[6] 2 Corinthians 5:17; John 3:17; John 5:24; and Hebrews 8:12.

Chapter Eight

REMOVING THE GRAVECLOTHES:
EMBRACING THE HELP OF A LOVING COMMUNITY

*Jesus said, "Take off the
grave clothes and let him go."*
—John 11:43

- We need others to help us in the process of transformation.
- We cannot expect community to give what only Jesus can give.
- Yet Jesus did not do what community is created to do.
- A transformational community is a resurrected community.

Jesus could have easily removed the graveclothes from Lazarus. The same power that resurrected Lazarus's body could have disintegrated the tightly wound graveclothes, allowing Lazarus to be free, indeed! Or, Jesus could have taken a few steps toward Lazarus, knelt before him, and then tenderly unwound the cloths one at a time. Instead Jesus asked the bystanders—the friends of Lazarus—to help remove the graveclothes that were wrapped around his body. "[You] take off the graveclothes and let him go." Jesus' intent is unmistakable: We are to help each other get rid of the things that hold us back in the spiritual life.

As I mentioned earlier, Gwen and I have a retreat in Colorado called Potter's Inn at Aspen Ridge. People come to this holy place to study, relax, talk, and learn about transformation and the care of the soul. The focal point of our ranch is a beautiful pastoral acreage where magnificent aspen trees grow.

Aspens are native to Colorado. Throughout this area the quaking leaves of these white barked trees make a rustling sound as the cool, dry air blows through the Rocky Mountains. In September when the leaves release their final tint of green, a pallet of gold and yellow erupts, drawing tourists from all over the world to marvel at the beauty.

You'll never find an aspen tree growing alone in a natural setting. Aspen trees grow in community. Their roots are intertwined under the ground, making a grove of trees into one big tree. In fact biologists have identified the largest living organism in the world as a huge, magnificent grove of aspens.

The story of Lazarus echoes the spiritual lesson of the aspen grove: We cannot grow alone. We were never meant to remain alone as we emerge from the tomb. As we learn from Lazarus, we see that our roots intertwine with others. Jesus calls us to embrace a "grove" of people and allow a community of friends to help us change.

A SOBERING CONFESSION

Here is something that is difficult for me to confess. My experience with community in the transformational process has not been what I thought it would be. Sometimes, in my darkest hours, I have wondered where my friends have gone. I have wondered if anyone really cares about me. At times in my life, I don't feel I am part of an aspen grove at all. I feel like a tender, young pine tree standing alone in a field.

Looking for Family

When I first became a follower of Jesus, I had high hopes for finding brothers and sisters, even fathers and mothers, who could help me grow as a new believer. The Christian language of family deeply appealed to me. It sounded like a place of belonging. I imagined times when the fatted calf would be roasted for the next few prodigals who arrived home. I looked for small groups, church meetings, and the fellowship of the "one anothers"[1] to offer me what I thought was the norm for the Christian experience of life.

I have found that I am not alone in my quest. Many of us are looking for the same thing. Yet our search for a place to belong and for a people to "do" life with often leaves us disappointed and disillusioned. No matter how hard we try, no matter how many places we look, friendship and community can be a superficial experience that never satisfies the soul.

We long for the deep friendships of David and Jonathan and Ruth and Naomi, but with the busyness of life, who has time to foster such friendships? What was meant to be community often turns into "catch up" times over coffee where we share safe stories of vacations and children.

What God has reminded me is that in every group, every family, and every church, people are wearing their own graveclothes. So am I. But I forget this so often, hoping that *this* group could be *the* place where I can finally deal with something important in my life, and all my needs will be met—finally.

But here's the deal: Rick wears his gravecloth of self-rejection every time we meet and chooses to not speak up or say anything important at all for the fear he has carried for years in his heart that people will laugh. Denise wears her gravecloth of blame and shame because she is not able to be regular at our group meeting. Her new job causes her to travel several days a week and her schedule is very unpredictable. She has told someone she is thinking about dropping out of the group because she "feels so bad." Rita is new in her faith and loves to quote the Bible even if she is interrupting one of us or changing the topic of discussion. She often wants to share "a word from the Lord" but is oblivious to the needs of those around her. Jim comes sporadically. He works late and hates his job. He can't talk about it in the group because our newest group member, Jeannie, works for the same company and feels her job is an "answer to prayer." I come to the group with my own past hurts, hesitant to trust others for fear of more disappointment.

We each bring something that hinders us. Yet we set high standards for others—and arrive at work, church, and the breakfast table with expectations that often lead to disappointment. So over the years we develop a long litany of disappointments with people. With that litany comes a hesitation about taking this crucial step in the transformation process. We play it safe by learning the correct doctrine—knowing the truth about Jesus but falling short of experiencing the intimacy of oneness with one another. Remembering the fact that each of us is wearing some form of a gravecloth helps replace criticism with compassion and judgment with understanding.

Yanking Off Bandages

When our youngest son Leighton was recovering from several abdominal surgeries following a ruptured appendix, he had special nurses who were trained in wound care and who spent what seemed like exorbitant time taking off the bandages. They first applied special ointments to chemically disintegrate the adhesives that held the bandages to his surgical wounds. They knew that pulling too much could cause even greater pain than their careful work already caused. Even now, if you ask my son his memories of spending thirty-one days in intensive care to recover from a ruptured appendix, the painful bandage removal following the surgery holds the worst memory for him.

Sometimes, when friends try to help each other in the spiritual life, we hurt more than we help. Maybe the gravecloth of someone else makes us uncomfortable, so we try to yank it off. Maybe we pull so insensitively that we expose more filthy rags underneath the first layer and cause shame. In our efforts to help people be free of their graveclothes, we end up making others feel guilty for being in a tomb in the first place.

A woman told me about an experience when her smelly graveclothes became too much for a small group Bible study to handle. Her group was studying verses about how God will never leave us nor forsake us. The group leader was doing a great job in leading through verse after verse, pointing out how true it is that God will not leave us in a bind.

Things went south in the group when this beautiful woman in her mid-thirties raised her hand to make a comment. She said, "All of these verses are beautiful to read and to think about, but [and here came the bombshell] when I was a five-year-old girl in the Midwest, every summer I spent two weeks with my grandparents. A cousin would come and take me into an outbuilding where he sexually molested and abused me. This happened every summer for several years. Where do you think God was when I was in the woodshed? Why didn't He protect me? Why didn't He show up?"

After an awkward moment of silence, the group leader said, "That's too bad. Thank you for sharing.... Our time is about up here. Let's come back next week when we'll focus on God's sovereignty." He closed in prayer, and when the group disbanded to go home, everyone shuffled their papers and seemed to make a special effort to talk to someone other than this woman. Instead of feeling acknowledged for her legitimate question, she felt unheard, and even ashamed, because of what she'd said.

Another friend of mine, who is divorced, told us of her experience recently when she visited a new church. She noticed an announcement for an "Ice Cream Social for All Pairs and Spares." Someone no doubt had good intentions to include singles in this fellowship time, but my friend lamented to us that the word *spares* made her cringe. She felt her newfound singleness would not be understood in that church if she was relegated to being a "spare." She never went back, fearing the community would aggravate old wounds.

We often try to fix people by quoting a Bible verse or telling them about a book we've read. We try to yank off the bandages or ignore the ones we don't want to face. When someone describes a past or current pain, we try to put a positive spin on it instead of simply listening. When we realize how much we do this ourselves, we can see why we have such a hard time finding a community that works.

Adjusting Our Expectations

None of us seizes every opportunity we can to be the friend we want to be to others. We have guilt about this. Hurt about that. Sin abounds. Yet we still want to try to be friends. And we should.

The most important thing to remember as we explore what it means to be in community is that friends cannot be to us what only Jesus can be. At times I have placed my highest expectations on the wrong people. I've expected my friends to save me and forgotten that Jesus is my Savior.

A community, no matter how wonderful, is simply not Jesus. So how do we seek out community knowing we will probably experience some level of disappointment? How do we hold realistic expectations and still hope for more? Knowing all the pitfalls and weaknesses of community, what could Jesus have meant when he told the people to help free Lazarus?

BUILDING A TRANSFORMATIONAL COMMUNITY

One Italian artist, Mattia Preti, painted a close-up scene of the raising of Lazarus in the 1650s. In the painting we see Lazarus sitting up on a slab of rock right outside the tomb. His resurrection has just happened and his transformation is taking place. He is half-asleep or half-alive, still obviously stunned over what has just happened. He has not moved much, but it's clear he's about to move closer to Jesus. He seems to be resting for a moment by the tomb's entrance.

As you look down at Lazarus's extended bare legs, you see a man untying Lazarus from a cord that had been wrapped around him. He has the cord in his right hand. He is looking at Jesus but is also aware of the gravecloth he is about to untie. He is gently, tenderly, and lovingly helping Lazarus free. Oh, for such a friend.

We cannot underestimate the importance of this kind of tenderness in community. Despite all the ways others can hurt us, we need one another in order to move forward in the spiritual life. In the story of Lazarus, Jesus did not do what community was meant to do. Jesus asked the community to take the graveclothes off Lazarus. He asks us to do the exact same thing within our own communities, families, and groups. This is one of the greatest purposes of Christian community: to show up for each other and to reach out and help one another in the process of being transformed. It takes community for this to happen. No one can untie his or her own graveclothes.

Of course, not all groups, classes, and even churches are intended to help one another in the transformational journey. Some groups are more social in nature. But a community that embraces transformation as a high value doesn't just happen. It needs to be fostered, modeled, and embraced.

Gwen and I work with a remarkable small group within a large denominational church in a Southern city. For over twenty years this transformational community has met regularly to free each other of graveclothes. This community has stood with one another through the births of their children, the deaths of their parents, job loss, marital affairs, and aging. They are living proof to us that healing transformation can take place when the graveclothes of each other are tended to with love, grace, and truth. They have been changed by the grace of God and the love of people—two important and vital ingredients in the journey toward transformation.

This group places a high value on each person's story. They ask good questions of each other. They provide a safe place to do the work of transformation. They invest time and love by protecting and prioritizing their fellowship with one another.

Listen to Paul's plea for us to have this kind of healthy community in each group and place:

> If you've gotten anything at all out of following Christ,
> if his love has made any difference in your life, if being
> in a community of the Spirit means anything to you,
> if you have a heart, if you care—then do me a favor:
> Agree with each other, love each other, be deep-spirited
> friends. Don't push your way to the front; don't sweet-
> talk your way to the top. Put yourself aside, and help
> others get ahead. Don't be obsessed with getting your
> own advantage. Forget yourselves long enough to lend
> a helping hand. (Phil. 2:1–4 msg)

Paul was writing to a group of people who were *trying* to help each other but got sidetracked from time to time in petty differences, doctrinal disagreements, and strong personalities. His encouragement to "put yourself aside, and help others get ahead" is striking. Evidently some of the members were lagging behind in shedding their graveclothes while others were doing quite well in their newfound freedom in Christ.

True community, Paul reminds us, is more than one person getting free. To be a transformational community, we need to serve each other in each person's individual journey. A community that is transformational is actually a community that is incarnational—one in which the members offer the hands, feet, and love of Jesus to one another.

Community might take the form of a church small group, a one-on-one relationship, or a group of close friends. Whatever form they take, healthy communities are places where resurrection is possible.

A healthy community is a safe community.
In 2 Kings 6:24–33, we read of a king who wore two layers of clothing. On the outside he wore his kingly robe of purple majesty. But underneath he wore sackcloths—the symbol of deep, personal turmoil and anguish. Underneath the image of power and prestige, this king was brokenhearted and ashamed. Yet no one knew. He had covered up the way he really felt. He created a false self—a self-made image of the person he wanted to present. This was not the true story of who he really was.

If everyone smells clean and looks clean, most likely you are not in a place of transformation. A community that seeks to help its members experience authentic transformation should be one where graveclothes and sackcloths are welcome. We can deny the realities of the messiness of life and pretend that we can hide our private stench. But Lazarus shows us a better way—a more life-giving way.

Recently a couple came to our retreat hoping for a time of restoration. In our first meeting the man blurted out: "I feel like I'm not a Christian. I'm not free. I am so bound by guilt and shame that I feel like I am going to die." He needed a place to finally open his heart after years of covering it up. He took the risk to be vulnerable in order to move forward in his longing for transformation.

As we have seen, information alone does not transform people. Study might be a part of our community, but vulnerability is an even more important part. Vulnerability means a certain kind of soul nakedness. Sharing your own stench allows others to share theirs. Who feels safe in the presence of perfection? Feeling safe leads to being real. It requires mutual sharing, not just one-way listening or talking.

A healthy community shares its stories.

Smelly people want to be listened to. Throughout my years dealing with my own stenches and the smells of others, I have become convinced of this. Just being able to share our stories brings healing. When we are listened to with love, we feel accepted, not judged and not put into a box. A listening ear becomes a sacred place to process our deeply held longings, fears, and dreams. Good questions become tools that God uses to help us know ourselves more. Asking good questions can be more important than learning the right answers. One of Jesus' primary teaching styles was asking good questions.

Exploring the soul of another person means being willing to face the unknown of what might lie underneath his smiling face. It means having the courage to look under a rock and see what might be there. In fact *courage* means "heart" in French. Having courage means having the heart to enter another person's heart, resisting the temptation to fix what you see or give advice. Good probing questions help each other become more aware of one's self and God.

A healthy community is full of grace.

A woman came to me who was active in a Christian fellowship where "truth-telling" had a high value. Sadly this group understood "truth-telling" to be the regular practice of telling each other what was really on their minds, including what really bothered them about people in the group. After she shared her experiences, I replied, "Sounds like you've had too much truth with not enough grace." That seemed to help her find a much-needed balance in her perspective on the group.

Our model for this balance is Jesus Himself. John tells us that Jesus was "full of grace and truth" (John 1:14). Too much grace might allow graveclothes to remain on too long. Too much truth can create even deeper wounds. Jesus' style was a life-giving balance of both grace and truth.

Many of us carry scars from groups, churches, and organizations where judgment, condemnation, and rebuke dominated, rather than the extravagant love and grace that Jesus modeled for us. People who are wounded know when they are just being tolerated. They tend to feel like they are a problem just because they showed up. In a grace-filled community, wounded, weary, and beat-up pilgrims are welcomed and wanted. It's not the healthy who need the Healer, but the sick.

A healthy community extends true hospitality.
Hospitality goes much deeper than offering oatmeal cookies on china dishes. We live in a fast-paced, busy, violent world. The pressure to meet quotas, perform, and achieve success seems to require that we live at a manic pace. We are often left breathless, overwhelmed, and spiraling. Our spiritual lives can mimic the demands of our professional lives. The need to do more, read more, and attend more events leaves us flailing in whitewater, navigating the rocks and jagged edges that rip into us every day.

Henri Nouwen reminds us that "hospitality is not to change people, but to offer them space where change can take place."[2] The word *hospitality* refers to a place where a guest comes, or where a weary traveler can rest. Our English word *hospital* has its roots in this concept—a place where wounded people come to get well. The spiritual journey is long and arduous, and we all need places where we can find a respite for our souls. A transformational community is one where the man or woman wearing graveclothes is given a place to rest.

Jesus gave us valuable insight into our need to be people of hospitality in his famous parable about the Good Samaritan. The unwanted, marginalized victim was passed by the religious right and overlooked by the professional clergy. The wounded man needed a person who knew what rejection felt like. It took someone who understood the pain of being dismissed and sidelined. It took a Samaritan, who the Jews disdained, to show us what Jesus meant by hospitality. Here's what Jesus said of the Good Samaritan:

> A Samaritan traveling the road came on him. When he saw the man's condition, *his heart went out to him.* He gave him *first aid, disinfecting and bandaging his wounds.* Then he lifted him onto his donkey, led him to an inn, and *made him comfortable.* In the morning he took out two silver coins and gave them to the inn-keeper, saying, *"Take good care of him.* If it costs any more, put it on my bill—I'll pay you on my way back." (Luke 10:33–35 MSG).

Here we see the cost of being a person who offers true hospitality. The Good Samaritan got involved physically in the dirty, perhaps smelly process of treating the wounds. He gave of his own resources when he provided money to the innkeeper. By pledging to return, he demon-strated his personal involvement in the healing process. He would come back to the inn to follow up.

Many people on the journey toward being transformed can relate to the feeling of being passed by and alone, unable to find the twenty-first-century equivalent to a healing inn.[3] Don't we all want places where we can sit down, process the journey, and gain new direction for our lives? Surely these are places where transformation happens.

A healthy community practices acceptance.
Acceptance means striving to accept others as Christ has accepted you. Acceptance acknowledges the fact that people are in process and will stumble on the way to transformation. Acceptance means becoming a welcoming person, not a gatekeeper. A gatekeeper of a group, church, or system is a person who does a sniff test to determine if someone will "fit." Being an accepting community means no gates keep the outsiders out.

As Paul writes in Romans 15:7: "Accept one another, then, just as Christ accepted you, in order to bring praise to God." Having an accepting posture in our hearts frees us to be like Jesus to others. We never see Jesus dismissing, marginalizing, or sidelining a person in the Gospels. He knew that accepting others was the mark of transforming love. Acceptance means simply this: We all have graveclothes. There are no exceptions. Each one of us can help another become more free, more alive, more ready to experience a life of resurrection.

A RESURRECTION COMMUNITY

After we emerge from the tomb, we have the incredible opportunity to experience community differently than before. The tomb has taught us a lot. The Voice of Love continues to speak individually to us. In community we benefit from all that we have experienced and all that we long for together. A small band of ordinary men and women are themselves transformed from a simple group to a resurrected community.

Transformed by God's love, we have greater purpose, greater insight, greater desire, and a greater journey ahead. This shared journey together lets us taste the life we all want. As Easter people—men and women who have experienced new life—we then walk forward. Our aloneness is assuaged. Our community is life giving. We form a circle of resurrected people with the same desire to know Jesus more.

A PRAYER FOR A RESURRECTED COMMUNITY

> *Jesus, please don't send me friends who will hold their noses when they smell my graveclothes! Give me people who know the stink and still love me. Send me people who will not cause greater pain by ripping at my graveclothes but will lovingly unbind me. Show me people who can get me to Jesus. Reveal to me compassionate hearts to understand me, loving ears to listen to me, truthful tongues and yet lips of grace. Let me do the same for them. Show me yourself in other people who are more like you than like me, people who marvel at your power of transformation and kneel at Your feet and not my own. Give me friends to make me laugh and friends who know my tears are sacred. Give me Jesus in the flesh even as You remind me that only through Jesus will I be transformed. Amen.*

NOTES

[1] The "one anothers" is a term used for the more than fifty times that the New Testament writers appeal for us to live in community with one another. "Love one another" is a term offered many times in the Bible. "Teach one another"; "Confess your sins to one another"; and "Encourage one another" are among the many examples given us by the biblical writers.

[2] Henri Nouwen, *Reaching Out* (New York: Image, Doubleday, 1975), 72.

[3] This story is a powerful and shaping force in my own life to offer such a place for people that we now call "The Potter's Inn."

Chapter Nine

LIVING IN THE LIGHT:
THE POWER OF YOUR TRANSFORMATION

*Six days before the Passover, Jesus
arrived at Bethany where Lazarus lived …*

—John 12:1

- A transformed life is a life of intimacy with Jesus.
- A transformed life is a life of gratitude and generosity.
- A transformed life is a life of danger.
- A transformed life is a life of influence.

When we leave John 11:44, we see Lazarus walking out of the tomb in his graveclothes. But his story does not end there. Neither does the influence of what God did through his life.

As the news spread about this transformed life—this resurrected life—many people who heard of Lazarus put their faith in Jesus. The lingering, the tomb, the smell, and the graveclothes all served to bring glory to God. But with the glory always comes danger. Always. And this is what happened to Lazarus. A transformed life can be threatening— the chief priests and the Pharisees saw Jesus' power and plotted to kill both Jesus and Lazarus (12:10). As a result Jesus "no longer moved about publicly among the Jews" (11:54).

It wasn't until six days before the Passover that Jesus returned to Bethany and the fellowship of his friends. Perhaps He arrived in the secrecy of the night. Can you feel the excitement of seeing Jesus again, of embracing the One who had brought new life to your family? "A dinner was given in Jesus' honor" to welcome Him (John 12:2).

In John 12 we're given a stunning glimpse into this dinner—and into what it means to live as a transformed person. Since this family at Bethany was ordinary, the house must have been ordinary as well, but still large enough to accommodate the disciples, Jesus, and the siblings. The five senses of each guest awakened that night and became "ministers to the soul," as Leonardo DaVinci once said. Tantalizing aromas filled the air. They had good food and great wine—perhaps the quality of the wine at the wedding feast John told us about earlier in his book. Mary and Martha offered the hospitality we show when someone special comes to our house for a visit. Sandals stayed at the door and bare feet felt the holiness of this dirt-floor home where Jesus would find refuge for an evening, just as he had many times before. Mary even poured an expensive container of perfume over Jesus' feet and then slowly wiped his feet clean with her hair, filling the room with fragrance.

Through all this, Jesus knew that his own tomb awaited him in just a few days. This dinner party was less than a week away from Jesus' own death. Imagine if you knew you only had one week to live. What would you do? Jesus chose to have a night of fellowship with His closest friends. This was not a night with an agenda. This was not a night to teach about evangelism. This was not a night of learning about heaven or hell. This was a night of intimacy. Companionship. This was a night of experiencing what life looks like in the presence of a God Who transforms.

A LIFE OF INTIMACY

We don't have many details of Lazarus's life after he was raised from the dead. But through John's eyes, we do not see Lazarus sharing his experience on a preaching tour. The first thing we read about Lazarus's actions after that day at the tomb is that he "was among those reclining at the table" with Jesus (12:2). The man once dead relaxes, fully alive in the presence of the God Who brought him back to life.

When people ate meals in the first century, they did not sit in chairs around a table. They reclined on the floor around a small, short table a few inches high and rested on cushions. Just as they do to this day in some Mideastern cultures, they leaned on their left arm and ate with their right hand. This was close communion! I can imagine

Lazarus scooting up right next to Jesus that night and staying beside Him. There was no sense of a lingering Jesus here. God was present. This was a home of joy. Imagine a dinner with the people you most love in life and you'll be close to experiencing what that night must have been like.

When I picture this scene, the first word that comes to mind is *intimacy*. It helps me to break that word down phonetically to gain an even deeper picture of what might have been happening: "into-me-see." Jesus would allow His friends to see His own heart. In return He would look deeply into theirs. Mary would wipe dripping oil from between the toes of God. Jesus would look into her face and love her for she was the beloved as well. We do not know much about the conversation at the table that night. We do know that these friends were basking in the simple presence of being together.

Alone with God

Intimacy with Jesus is a mark of a transformed life. Busyness is not. This truth calls us to swim against the forceful currents of the Christian culture that says: Do more! Be more involved! As Oswald Chambers reminds us, "the greatest competitor to our devotion to Jesus Christ is our service for him."[1]

When I became a Christian in college, well-meaning older Christians advised me to "go out and talk about Jesus" to others right away. In other words, *act, do, perform* to solidify my relationship with Jesus. I see the rationale behind their advice, but in retrospect it would have been more meaningful to me—and therefore led to deeper relationships with others in the end—if I had been encouraged to "withdraw" with

God for a while, just as Paul did after his conversion, just as Jesus did Himself many times.

In fact, immediately after Lazarus's resurrection, Jesus *"withdrew to a region near the desert, to a village called Ephraim, where he stayed with his disciples"* (11:54). In a remote place Jesus gathered his followers in a circle of love—another time of "into-me-see." He needed a safe place, as we all do at times.

It's taken me decades to realize that transformation does not always result in immediate action. Transformation might first lead to simply enjoying the presence of Jesus, a time that prepares us for the good work God calls us to do.

A time will come for action and engagement. We have no greater cause than sharing our faith with others—indeed, many people came to faith in Jesus because of the news of Lazarus's resurrection. But without times of joyful intimacy with Jesus, we will lose our way on the long path of transformation. We simply cannot endure this journey without frequent and meaningful times of fellowship with God, times when we're not *doing* anything but praying, listening, and simply being in the presence of the One who loves us for who we are.

Leaning in to Jesus

A life of intimacy with Jesus is not a passive life. At the same time, it's not necessarily a life of calm and quiet. In the rush of our days, we get the idea that *calm* is all we need to be closer to God. But the person seeking transformation cannot seek a life in a monastery unless he or she is called to do just that. Graveclothes follow us to monasteries, too. Having a day without a full schedule will not bring peace; an ongoing, intimate relationship with Jesus on busy and quiet days will bring peace. The rhythm of Jesus' life is the rhythm of a transformed life: a time of activity followed by a time of reflection. Both are vitally needed.

As Thomas R. Kelly writes in his spiritual classic, *A Testament of Devotion:*

> Over the margins of life comes a whisper, a faint call, a premonition of richer living which we know we are passing by. Strained by the very mad pace of our daily outer burdens, we are further strained by an inward uneasiness, because we have hints that there is a way of life vastly richer and deeper than all this hurried existence, a life of hurried serenity and peace and power.[2]

The Lazarus life is a life of "unhurried existence." We can be busy when we look calm, and we can also know a deep peace in the busiest moments of our day. The most important thing Lazarus did after his transformation was to lean next to Jesus. We must do the same.

A LIFE OF GRATITUDE AND GENEROSITY

The night of Jesus' party, Mary's heart burst with gratitude and generosity as she poured expensive perfume on Jesus' feet. This outpouring of gratitude and generosity is another mark of a transformed life, a sign that transformation is deep and lasting.

Mary did not use a watered-down, toilet-water kind of perfume that night. This perfume cost 300 denarii, the equivalent of a year's wages.

Imagine taking your entire salary this year and spending it in one night to show love to someone. Would you do that?

Others reclined at the table with Jesus that night. One of them was Judas, the man who would betray Jesus just a few days later. As the accountant for the group, Judas strongly objected to Mary's actions. It was extravagant. It was not necessary. Yet Jesus says to Judas, "Let her alone" (John 12:7 MSG). Jesus received Mary's act of devotion and expression of love. What looked like waste was actually a beautiful reflection of the power of transformation.

Then Jesus reveals that Mary had been saving this perfume. This was not a spontaneous act of irrational behavior. The three siblings who lived together probably discussed the gift as they prepared for the lavish feast. What should we give Jesus? What is the proper gift to show our gratitude? Mary had just the answer. She had seen Jesus live life. She watched Him with people. She noticed her own heart come alive in His presence. She grew closer to Him during a time of waiting for Him to arrive. Through her deep disappointment, Mary learned a deeper part of love that she did not know before. She saw Jesus live abundantly. She chose to do the same.

Gratitude marks a transformed life. When you experience a change that is beyond your own ability to acquire or manufacture it, a posture of humility and gratitude is all you have to offer. A transformed person moves in gratitude because she knows what has happened to her and she realizes she had nothing to do with it. After all, Jesus commended the man who had leprosy who came back to express his thanks. Nine others who were healed simply went on their way—enjoying health but without hearts humble and aware enough to remember the one who brought healing.

When we move forward out of our tombs, we take steps to becoming generous and grateful. Thanksgiving is practiced every day, not just once a year. Giving is natural for some people. For most of us, however, it is a discipline we need to practice. The discipline of giving generously means making space in our heart for a greater presence of God. As the money, energy, and time flow out, God becomes a richer presence in our lives. David once said, "I will not give to the Lord that which costs me nothing" (1 Chron. 21:24). Giving generously means sacrificing something important to us. When we give something that matters—something that is significant—we find that strangely, we are also given to. Sacrifice for God always brings us closer to Him.

Our graveclothes show up vibrantly in this area. In general, Americans give less than 2.2 percent of their income to benevolent causes. Americans whose annual income is greater than $150,000 give away 1.9 percent of the income. By contrast, people classed as the "working poor" give 10–15 percent their income on average.[3] Perhaps those who have the least money have the greatest humility. Their own experience has taught them a profound truth of transformation: When a heart beats only for itself, it is not a heart beating in sync with the giving heart of God.

Martin Luther once said that there are "three conversions necessary: the mind, heart, and the purse." What do you hate to waste? Time, expertise, abilities, money, words? Consider whether you are hoarding any of these things in your relationships with others and with God. Ordinary people can give in extraordinary ways because God touches their hearts.

Just as we see Jesus giving, we should give. Just as we see God pouring out his love for us, so our hearts should pour out for others. Paul reminds us to "Be imitators of God" (Eph. 5:1). As we grow in our transformation, we also grow in our desire to be Godlike. God modeled a lavish, giving heart.

A LIFE OF DANGER

While Jesus reclined at the table with His friends, a crowd gathered at the door. These people gathered not only to see Jesus but "also to see Lazarus, whom [Jesus] had raised from the dead" (12:9). Imagine becoming an instant celebrity in your hometown. Something so incredible has happened to you that people stare as you go about your daily work. People ask you questions and whisper among themselves when you walk by. Your transformation so defines you that people do not talk about you alone. They talk about you in relation to the fact that you have been transformed. You have become *identified* with the one who changed your life.

This is the experience of Lazarus. John tells us twice (11:46 and 12:10) that the religious leaders used this single experience of Lazarus's resurrection to build a conspiracy about Jesus. They manipulated truth to serve their own needs and orchestrated a plan that set things in motion for Jesus to be executed (11:53) and for Lazarus himself to be killed—to die yet again (12:10). Lazarus was now clearly identified with Jesus. And walking closely to Jesus can result in a dangerous life.

Transformation never occurs in a vacuum. Stepping out of that tomb will have repercussions we cannot imagine at the time. Remaining in the tomb is safer than emerging as a changed person. Change stirs fear in people. Change brings controversy. What should be celebrated is often shunned instead.

Letting go of old habits, changing how we relate to others, even breaking free from addictions will change our relationships. It might cause us to rethink some of our theological beliefs. It will change the way we talk and the "God-language" we use. Some people won't know how to react to our new commitment to Jesus. As we've discussed, some people will even try to get us to go back in the tomb. After all, one person emerging from a tomb might lead someone else to give up that safe life as well. One person revealing his graveclothes makes another realize that she doesn't smell so good herself.

Jesus Himself knew rejection, grief, loneliness, and harsh treatment as he lived out a life that was different than what people expected. A transformed life will not be immune from trials and woes. But the struggles that seem like dead ends can be the places of even deeper transformation. At the end of our journey we realize that being in the arms of God is, after all, the safest place to be.

A LIFE OF INFLUENCE

We live in a day where we hear no end of promised remedies that can cure the body and fix the soul. The most effective sales pitch for any pill, cookie, or shoe store is the personal testimony of someone who believes in the product. A similar reality happens in the spiritual life, with much more significant results.

After Lazarus's resurrection, "many of the Jews who had come to visit Mary, and had seen what Jesus did, put their faith in him" (11:45). The Voice of Love called more people than just Lazarus to Himself on that day. John tells us that after the dinner party, the word about

Lazarus's resurrection kept spreading to the point that the Pharisees complained that "the whole world has gone after" Jesus (12:17, 19).

When we are desperate for change in our lives, we look for something or someone to satisfy us. When we are convinced that a story of transformation is indeed true, we will consider changing where we place our faith, time, and money.

As Lazarus emerged from the tomb, each step forward became a dramatic step of influence in the hearts of those who watched. As we've seen, artistic renditions of that moment suggest that some bystanders fell to worship Jesus, some moved back in astonishment, and some covered their noses because of the stench. Everyone reacted in some way.

Lazarus's new life impacted the crowd. His story surely transformed his sisters. Its influence continues today, having a profound impact on a twenty-first century individual like me. For the past two years, I have read John 11 almost daily. The longer I have lived with Lazarus, the more I have benefited. Lazarus has become a friend to accompany me on my journey toward Jesus. The Lazarus life becomes a model for me, a top-of-the-box image of what the puzzle of transformation can look like for each one of us. Transformation is suddenly a distinct possibility.

The Power of Story

Several times each year I lead a retreat called, "The Transformation of a Man's Heart." It's based on a book I was privileged to work on a few years ago. In this retreat several ordinary men share their true stories of how they have been transformed in a specific area of life. One man will share about how his marriage has experienced transformation after years of infidelity; he will speak about the graveclothes of guilt and shame that he is going to leave at this year's retreat. Another will tell his story of giving up alcohol and restoring his relationships with his grown kids after years of intense gravecloth removal.

Jim, a dear friend of mine, decided at this retreat to begin spending quality time with his wife—something she had been asking him to do for years. Jim loved his wife but always wanted to do one more thing at work before spending time with her. At the retreat he shared with us a decision he made to move toward transformation. Jim doesn't like coffee and never has, but his wife does. In fact she often asked Jim to share a cup of coffee with her and just talk. Jim's decision was to begin this ritual together. Every day they would have a cup of coffee and read a short devotional together. Jim's decision is a simple step forward toward strengthening his marriage. (And now, Jim says, he actually likes coffee!)

At last year's retreat a group of older men, all over the age of sixty, stood and shared their heart-wrenching stories. There was not a dry eye in the auditorium. In the back of the room, a group of men in their twenties stood up and gave their senior brothers a rousing standing ovation. One person's transformation inspires others.

Transformation takes different forms in each of our lives. We have no formula to produce the kind of transformation we want, no twenty-one steps to a transformed life. We only have obedience to Jesus' call. Perhaps God knows that if we had a formula we would worship the formula instead of Him. Instead He calls us to the mysteries of the spiritual life. He asks us to listen to the stories of others and then receive the individual transformation He has for our own lives.

The writer of Hebrews tells us about a host of ordinary, transformed men and women and asks us to remember God's work in *their* lives. We're told to "keep your eyes on Jesus … When you find yourself flagging in your faith, go over that story again, item by item … That will shoot adrenaline into your souls" (Heb. 12:1–3 MSG). I love that line, "shoot adrenalin into your souls." That's how stories of transformation work. They energize us on our way to Jesus.

A true story of transformation opens our hearts to our own possibilities. We may not share the same problem as another person, but our journeys are similar in many ways. People who really change have something to say that hooks us. They act different because they *are* different. We find ourselves wanting what they experienced. We want Lazarus stories—real, touchable, visible. We want an invitation to experience transformation for ourselves.

LOOKING RESURRECTED

Once in a while, I have to admit, I pick up a magazine in the checkout line at the grocery store (don't you?). Many of those periodicals tell "transformation" stories of how someone lost weight, changed careers, or reconciled with family. After a quick scan of this kind of article, I simply wonder, *Is this person telling me the truth? If he is, maybe I can do the same thing he did. Maybe I should put my Snickers back before the cashier scans it.* It's a momentary civil war. I want to look like the "after" image, but I want my Snickers, too!

In the end what each of us wants is a true story of transformation. Nothing else will do. Fiction may make us weep but truth makes us want to change. We long to know that someone out there has experienced a life-changing breakthrough because that means it might be possible for us.

EXTRAORDINARY GOD

Maybe you are thinking that you are not a Mary who has perfume to pour out on Jesus' feet. Maybe you don't feel like a modern-day Lazarus. Is there hope for those of us who live ordinary lives—who work long hours in demanding jobs, who try to live the right way, who teach a class of children at church or volunteer at the food pantry or make lunches every evening for the kids to take to school the next day? Is there hope for the man who wants to honor God but feels inside like he's a charlatan? Is there hope for a woman with small children to find fulfillment when she feels like her life doesn't count?

This is why the story of Lazarus is so important for us to read. Lazarus was not a man like Abraham. He was not a king like David. He wrote no psalms and left no journal. He was not one of the twelve disciples. He did not go on a mission trip with Paul. He did not become a companion with Jesus on His way to the cross. He lived a small, simple, ordinary life in a small town called Bethany. Yet his experience with Jesus not only changed his life it changed the lives of those around him.

We may not see someone raised from the dead in our lifetime, but the miracles of Jesus are just as real in our homes today as they were in Bethany two thousand years ago. An ordinary life touched by God becomes a life of influence and power. God uses the former messes, stink, and graveclothes of our lives to help others experience transformation as well. So this is how a transformed life works: First we are transformed. Then God uses our own story to transform the lives of others.

Andy and Joanne's story is filled with the drama of a Hollywood movie, but it is true. They have been married now for thirty years. They married while attending a Christian college and then raised their family as active members of their community church. The outer story of their lives showed success, servant hearts, and involvement in church, tennis clubs, and the neighborhood.

The inner story showed a mess. Andy had several affairs over the years of their marriage. He tried each time to recover from the devastation and carnage. Then Andy's boss caught him with a secretary and Andy lost his job, the trust of his wife, and what seemed to be his life in one day. Joanne's life as she knew it ended as well. Everything changed.

Andy, Joanne, their oldest son, and their closest friends entered a dark and desperate tomb. Joanne says that she cried for a year every night wondering, *Why had this happened? What had I missed? Why did Andy do this to me? What was wrong with him—with me?* She deeply loved Andy, and though aware of her options to divorce him, she explored her own heart's brokenness and desperately wanted Andy to do the same. *Could Andy really change? Was it really over?* Their house of illusions came crashing down with a thud that rocked their church, school, and friends.

Andy and Joanne's journey of transformation reveals that hearts do change. They were encircled by fellow wounded hearts—men and women who themselves knew the stench of the tomb. For two years, three of these friends, two of whom were elders in the church, met every Wednesday evening with Andy and Joanne to talk about their emotions, disappointments, and the illusions of life they'd held without realizing it. This circle of love tended to the mess that kept oozing out of their wounded souls. Andy and Joanne began the slow work of transformation. They began to have hope that their love could somehow be rekindled—a love both of them wanted. They began to emerge from their dark tomb of certain death. Andy did personal work with a counselor, studied his own life, discovered his own soul-sickness, and become more God-aware and self-aware than ever before.

When I called Andy and Joanne to get permission to use their story here, they told me that today they feel "more alive than ever and more in love as well." Their church, committed to helping people transform their lives, has asked Joanne to serve as a leader in women's ministry. The pastor told Joanne, "Your main job is to tell your story and help the women with their own stories of transformation. Just be yourself and love the women well."

Andy also continues his journey. The loss of his job sent him into a professional tailspin and an economic loss that the family is still recovering from. Seven years later he is just beginning to see the end of the professional and financial turmoil.

Sam, the oldest of their three children, was in high school when his world collapsed. Deeply wounded and disappointed by his dad's actions, Sam sought his own help with a trusted professor at his college. Sam is now in graduate school preparing for a life of service to others.

He says he wants to be involved in the care of people's souls and is considering becoming a pastor. Sam's journey has not been an easy one. But he's been brave to face his own disillusionment head-on, refusing to live a life of shame and blame.

Andy and Joanne are now asked to share their remarkable story of transformation. It's dangerous because their youngest child does not know the mess her parents have lived. It's dangerous because of what a story like this can do if not shared well. It's dangerous because now, Andy and Joanne don't want to live a life of pretense. They want a life that really is a life. They only feel safe sharing the details to groups and couples where they have built trust, authenticity, and safety.

Andy and Joanne are modern-day Lazaruses: ordinary people who loved God but whose lives imploded and who said "life for us is now over as we have known it." And in many ways their former lives really did end.

Now the fruit of transformation is budding around them. Their lives are being used to inspire others to believe that true change is possible. Having given up the illusion of the perfect marriage, now they experience a transformed one. Their jarring and brokenness resulted in coming alive again. Their tomb was the birthplace of transformation. Their marriage is a place for intimacy with each other like they have never known before. Their hearts are the place to experience a new love.

Some of us might say, "I would have left my spouse for doing that to me!" Yes, some of us would. But because Joanne lived through the messy process of transformation in her marriage, she herself has changed. She knows for a fact that Andy has changed as well. Now she says, "I would never go back to the life I had. It was no life at all compared to what I know now." Andy says the same thing.

Andy and Joanne's story is not so dramatic that you and I cannot find the everyday power of transformation in it. The journey of this one couple simply reflects the life we want and need. As we will explore in the next chapter, this is, after all, Jesus' greatest promise.

NOTES

[1]　Chambers, *My Utmost for His Highest*, 18.

[2]　Thomas R. Kelly, *A Testament of Devotion* (New York: HarperOne, 1996), 92.

[3]　As reported on *20/20*, ABC Television and Excellence in Giving in Colorado Springs, CO (September 14, 2007).

Chapter Ten

THE LAZARUS LIFE:
EXPERIENCING TRANSFORMATION FOR A LIFETIME

*Jesus said, "I am the
resurrection and the life."*
—John 11:25

- Is the life you're living the life you want to live?

The greatest spiritual question we can ask ourselves is not, "Is there life after death?" The real question is much deeper: "Is there life *before* death? Or at least more than I've been living?" The story of Lazarus offers us the answer. We need look no further than the most quoted line from his story—the line we hear at the gravesides of our friends and family: *I am the resurrection and the life.* But the graveside is not the only place we need to hear such riveting words. We need to hear them now, before it's too late to live the one life we have been given. Famed novelist Victor Hugo has reminded us: "It is nothing to die; it is dreadful not to live." Lazarus helps us to face what is frightful and to embrace the journey that leads to real life.

Let's back up in the story for a moment. When Jesus finally arrived in Bethany, Martha was still resentful and disappointed. Even so, she knew that Lazarus "will be raised up in the resurrection at the end of time" (11:24 MSG). Mary probably believed the same as well. But Jesus wasn't talking about the end of time; He was talking about the now. Jesus had *more* to offer the sisters right then and there. And He has *more* to offer us.

- What is the *more* that you dream for your life?
- What is the *more* that you want?
- What is the *more* that you need?
- Are you having trouble even answering these questions?

Earlier in John's gospel Jesus said He came to give us *abundant* life. The abundant life is the life of "more"—it is the resurrected life. When we read Jesus' words in John 10:10 in different translations, we gain a deeper sense of the life He wants his followers to have:

- I have come that they may have life, and *have it to the full.* (NIV)
- My purpose is to give them *a rich and satisfying life.* (NLT)
- I came that they may have and *enjoy life,* and have it in *abundance (to the full, till it overflows).* (AB)
- I came so they can have *real and eternal life, more and better life than they ever dreamed of.* (MSG)

This theme of "life" permeates the writings of John the apostle. He goes to great lengths to make certain that we are very clear as to the source of this abundant life: Jesus. And nothing else. Not surprising, though, from the disciple whom Jesus *loved:*

- "In him (Jesus) was *life*" (John 1:4).
- "Everyone who believes in him (Jesus) may have eternal *life* (3:15).
- "Whoever believes in the Son (Jesus) has eternal *life* (3:36).
- "You (Jesus) have the words of eternal *life* (6:68).
- "This is the real and eternal *life*: that they know you, the one and only true God (17:3 MSG).
- "These are written down so you will believe that Jesus is the Messiah, the Son of God, and in the act of believing, have *real and eternal life* in the way he personally revealed it" (20:31 MSG).[1,2]

In the midst of competing sources of life today, only Jesus gives real life. Life is being in proximity to Jesus. It's about being close to Jesus. In a sense Lazarus had never been closer to Jesus than when he came out of the tomb. Take a look at the painting again. Lazarus's face is set. He knows exactly where he's going—he's headed toward Jesus. The closer we are to Jesus, the more life we experience. Jesus and life are the same. There—in the closeness to Jesus—in the step-by-step movement toward Him, we can see what is going to happen. Lazarus is going to live like he's never lived before! Jesus offered Lazarus what the world cannot—LIFE! He offers us the same now!

Apart from Jesus we know little about this life except skewed perspectives about survival of the fittest, dying with the most toys, and if anything starts to sag, a surgeon out there can lift it. But life is more than survival, more than hoarding, and certainly more than youth.

What is most important, most desired, most longed for, and most needed is found in Jesus. This is the message that Lazarus finally heard and it is the same one we must hear if we have any hope of real life. Open the ears of our hearts, Lord.

THERE'S MORE

But saying yes to the "more" means saying no to the "less than"; the counterfeit voices that promise resurrection but don't deliver. It's amazing how easily we're convinced that these counterfeit voices are the real thing. Do you find yourself listening to lies and making choices that ignore these truths?

There is more to life than my work.
Competing voices will fool us into thinking that power and life—even abundant life—can be found in what we do rather than who we are.

There is more to life than another person.
A spouse, friend, child, or parent becomes our resurrection and life when we focus our needs, desires, and dreams on him or her.

There is more to life than money.
When our sense of significance is attached to money, our true identity is compromised and our integrity hangs in the balance. Jesus gave money a rival god status. We should do the same.

There is more to life than sex.
We live in a culture fixated on sex. This brokenness stems from human hearts that are desperate to be loved. There is a difference between "having sex" as an act and expressing our hearts to our spouses as the Beloved of God.

There is more to life than church.
Even church can become a substitute for true resurrection and life if we are not careful. Our cultural fascination with size, power, and prestige influences our perception of Christian communities. As we have seen, fellowship with others is a crucial part of our spiritual growth. But Jesus never said that church would be our life. Had He meant that, surely He would have mentioned the word *church* more than the couple of times He spoke about it.[3]

Every day offers us the choice to decide what will be our source of life. Poet David Whyte reminds us that "sometimes we must *unmake* a living in order to get back to living the life we wanted for ourselves."[4]

What needs to be unmade in our lives? To have the life that Jesus is describing will inevitably require that we "unmake," or change, our ways—which is the literal meaning of the word *repent*. The journey to Jesus requires that we *repent* more than one time in our life. We will need to change our direction and our ways many times on the journey to Jesus.[5] As it was Martha's choice to believe Jesus, it is ours as well. How we choose determines the quality of the life we will live.

> Let's take a good look at the way we're living and reorder our lives under God. (Lam. 3:40 MSG)

Maybe we have schedules that are too full, commitments that are life-draining, relationships filled with disappointment and pain. You and I may or may not be able to change these life-realities. But it may be that the Lazarus story has revealed something that needs to be reordered—transformed—in our lives. It may be that taking the steps of the Lazarus life explored in this book can help "unmake" the power of difficult realities as we move forward.

I ask again: Is the life you're living the life you want to live?

THREE-DOLLAR GOSPEL

Far too many of us are living a somewhat stable life, yet we are unfulfilled. Like insatiable consumers we look for a little bit of this and a little bit of that to satisfy our deepest aches. D. A. Carson wrote a piece titled *Three Dollars Worth of the Gospel*. I fear many of us want about three dollars worth of the resurrection. Here's how he describes the kind of life some of us might find ourselves seeking, whether we are conscious of it or not:

> I would like to buy about three dollars worth of gospel, please.
>
> Not too much—just enough to make me happy, but not so much that I get addicted.
>
> I don't want so much gospel that I learn to really hate covetousness and lust.
>
> I certainly don't want so much that I start to love my enemies, cherish self-denial, and contemplate missionary service in some alien culture.
>
> I want ecstasy, not repentance;
>
> I want transcendence, not transformation.
>
> I would like to be cherished by some nice, forgiving, broad-minded people, but I myself don't want to love those from different races—especially if they smell.
>
> I would like enough gospel to make my family secure and my children well behaved, but not so much that I find my ambitions redirected or my giving too greatly enlarged.
>
> I would like about three dollars worth of the gospel, please.[6]

Here's my paraphrase of Carson's words, focusing on the resurrection:

> I would like about three dollars worth of the resurrection, please.
>
> I want enough to be alive—but not so much that I may have to get too close to Jesus.
>
> I certainly don't want so much resurrection that I'll have a family of other gravecloth-wearing brothers and sisters to belong to instead of a church to attend.
>
> I want the comfort of the Lord's Prayer, but not the intimacy of the Father-God.
>
> I want a get-out-of-jail-free card, not transformation.
>
> I would like a higher standard of living, but not if it means I would have to do what the rich, young ruler refused to do.
>
> I would like enough resurrection to get out of the tomb, but I really don't have any desire to do the hard work of removing my graveclothes.
>
> I'm thinking I want to thrive, but maybe just surviving will do.
>
> I would like about three dollars worth of the resurrection, please.

What will three dollars get you? Not much. Certainly, not life. There is more! How do I know? I speak as a man living the Lazarus life.

TELLING

I must tell you how Jesus has brought "more" into my relationship with my father and mother and transformed broken places within my fragile soul. You'll recall that nicks and wounds received in my formative years and primary relationships have left me limping, hobbled by graveclothes throughout my life. At times I have wondered if I would ever be free from the wrappings that have felt like chains around my heart.

I need to tell you that over the years, aided by the gentle hands of friends who have reached for the frayed edge of my graveclothes, I have found more freedom and more healing than I imagined possible. It's felt like genuine transformation! Raw emotions of anger, disappointment, and bitterness have now been transformed by love's alchemy into a precious knowing that I was truly loved. And I am truly loved. It has looked different than I thought it would, but this has been my own journey toward living life NOW. But I have only told you of transformation. Now let me show you.

SHOWING

Just a few years ago, when I was in my mid-40s, I went back to my parents' house for a visit. This was not a response to some parental summons, but a man's attempt to put away childish ways. When I greeted my then eighty-year-old mother, I asked her to stand up, and as I helped her aged body rise, I took her arms and placed them around my waist, holding them there for a moment. And there it was, a moment of transformation, a healing embrace. My little soul inside my big body was being held like I had always wanted to be. This hug of transformation brought my heart just what it needed. It may seem small, but it was one more step away from the tomb.

I surprised my mother with that action. I decided to make a similar, but different effort toward healing the gulf between my father and me. I asked my father to meet me one day for lunch. This lunch would be "more" than a lunch. I had a list of questions I wanted to work through with him. I suggested a very plain restaurant about equal distance for both of us; I was trying to meet the man halfway. We each ordered soup and suddenly the scene resembled so many mornings of sitting at the breakfast table with my father and his silence. But intentional efforts at transformation can break history's repetitive spell; this day would be different. There would be more.

My words were courage-filled, my heart was racing: "Dad, before you die, there are some things I need to hear from you." I thought it was a fair statement, one that seemed to me to present an open avenue of discussion. But I was not prepared for his response. He leaned back in his chair as if to posture his body for what he might have perceived to be an attack and said, "Steve, before *YOU* die, there are some things I need to hear from you." I was totally caught off guard, cut off at the pass. He had somehow managed to do an end-run around my heart and surprised me with a question I was never prepared to face.

I momentarily sat in stunned silence. But courage prevailed. I said, "Okay. Seems like we both need to hear something from the other. I'll go first." After pausing and swallowing yet another lump in my throat, I said, "I need to hear you say, 'Steve, I love you.'" I then proceeded to stir my soup bowl as feverishly as a man stirs wet concrete when preparing to pour it. Oh, that my heart would not be set like concrete …

He said the words unashamedly. Unapologetically. Unadorned. But courageously. "Steve, I do love you." He paused and then asked, "Now, can you tell me that you love me?"

I was immediately struck by the lesson from my friend Lazarus: We are all struggling to emerge from the tomb. Evidently, in my own soul-sickness for love over the course of my life, I had not spoken the words he most needed to hear with *meaning* and *conviction*. I guess he had always heard those three words out of my own obligation; perhaps only from a responsible son indebted for his physical needs. My father and I were crying out for the same thing, the only thing that truly transforms. Love.

My mother's arms around my waist. My father's words over a bowl of soup. The desperately needed words of his son spoken in return. Whatever form love takes, it is still the only thing that transforms the soul-sickness of our hearts. It is what Lazarus needed. It is what my father and I needed. It is what our world needs. Now.

I speak as a man living the Lazarus life. These small acts of love nourished a love that I have always been hungry for. In boyish ways I looked and searched in various places. As a man I hunted in others. Life was nourished between us that has felt like something being resurrected between us. Now there is an understanding. Peace. Acceptance. It's not been something I could have mustered up. It's been like being given the chance to truly live again, to love again; to live as a transformed, ordinary man.

WHAT ARE YOU LIVING FOR?

Thomas Merton writes, "Ask me not what I eat or where I live. Ask me what it is I live for and what it is that keeps me from living fully for that." Don't move too quickly away from Merton's questions. Sit with them for a while before reading on.

What are you living for? Is the life you're living the life you want to live?

Perhaps your answer reveals a tomb more than it reveals a life marked by resurrection. Do you believe lies about yourself that are keeping you from experiencing the resurrected life? What is preventing you from living fully the life Jesus wants for you? Remember, a life of transformation involves becoming more God-aware and more self-aware at the same time. This awareness breathes life, not death. This is the awareness that leads to resurrection. This is the "more."

It should not sound like a luxury to ask such questions. They are some of the most important questions we will ever ask, questions that remind us we can still make adjustments since the work of transformation is ongoing.

After all, transformation is a gift. It is a gift because it is something God does, not something we do. Lazarus initially did nothing but hear the Voice of Love. This chance to redo, rethink, and remake reflects the matchless grace of God. My own soul-sickness is being transformed. Yours can be too! We get one life but many opportunities in this one life to get it right. To live a transformed life is a life-long privilege.

DO YOU BELIEVE?

Jesus' words to Martha were an invitation to more, an invitation to live. They were not words spoken to the dead Lazarus, but rather the living Martha. Her heart must have been racing, her lungs must have been gasping for breath in seeing Jesus finally arrive. But perhaps Martha had only been existing.

This is why Jesus pressed Martha. This is why Jesus would not accept her doctrinal confession. This is why Jesus asked her the most important question possible: "Do you believe this? (11:26).

Lazarus's life is our life. His story is our story! And Martha's question is our question: *Do you believe this?* Do you believe what you've seen and heard of the ordinary man named Lazarus? Do you believe that our life—the life God dreamed for us—is a life of ongoing, step-by-step transformation? Do you believe that the journey matters as well as the destination in the spiritual life? Do you believe that there's more to this life? Right now? And His name is Jesus? Do you believe that if you are banking on the afterlife to *finally* live, you will be choosing to live a life differently from the life of Lazarus and Jesus?

Martha answered her question. I am answering mine. Only you can answer yours. Listen. Do you hear that? It is the Voice of Love calling: "Come forth, I love you. I know, it's not easy, but I'll be with you. Friends will help too. I know you don't think you can, but trust Me.

Yes, it will hurt, but I love you. The life I promised you is waiting. Keep stumbling forward. I love you. I always have."

God is kind, but he's not soft.
In kindness he takes us firmly by the hand
and leads us into radical life-change.
(Rom. 2:4 MSG)

NOTES

[1] Later, John writes in 1 John these words about the source of life: "He who has the Son (Jesus) has life; he who does not have the Son of God does not have life" (1 John 5:12).

[2] For other references in John's writings about "life" see: John 1:4, 3:15–16, 3:36, 5:24, 5:40, 6:63, 6:68, 10:10, 11:25, 14:6, 17:3, 20:31; 1 John 1:1–3, 2:25, 5:11–12. Throughout John's Revelation, John refers to the "book of Life" as a document containing all the names of the people who will live.

[3] The only times Jesus spoke the word *church* are found in Matthew 16:18—"I will build my church."—and 18:17.

[4] David Whyte, *Crossing the Unknown Sea*, (New York: Riverhead Books, 2001), 77.

[5] The hymn writer said it this way, "Prone to wander, Lord, I feel it. Prone to leave the God I love." Isaac Watt described it this way:

"O to grace how great a debtor
Daily I'm constrained to be!
Let that grace now, like a fetter,
Bind my wandering heart to Thee.
Prone to wander, Lord, I feel it,
Prone to leave the God I love;
Here's my heart, O take and seal it,

Seal it from Thy courts above."

Watt's words describe a new kind of binding that must happen; not with graveclothes but with the cords of love and grace.

6 D. A. Carson, *Basics for Believers: An Exposition of Philippians* (Grand Rapids, MI: Baker Academics, 1996), 12–13.

For more information, group resources, and ideas
to explore related to *The Lazarus Life*, please go to:

www.lazaruslife.com

On the Web site, you can find music ideas, a gallery of art based on
Lazarus, video clip ideas, blog, sermon/talk outlines and more!

Potter's Inn is a Christian ministry founded by Stephen W. and Gwen Harding Smith, and is dedicated to the work of spiritual formation. A resource to the local church, organizations, and individuals, Potter's Inn promotes the themes of spiritual transformation to Christians on the journey of spiritual formation by offering

- guided retreats
- soul care
- books, small group guides, works of art, and other resources that explore spiritual transformation.

Steve and Gwen travel throughout the United Stages and the world offering spiritual direction, soul care, and ministry to people who long for deeper intimacy with God. Steve is the author of *Embracing Soul Care: Making Space for What Matters Most* and *Soul Shaping: A Practical Guide to Spiritual Transformation*.

Potter's Inn at ASPEN RIDGE Potter's Inn at Aspen Ridge is a thirty-five-acre ranch and retreat nestled in the Colorado Rockies near Colorado Springs, Colorado. As a small, intimate retreat, Potter's Inn at Aspen Ridge is available for individual and small group retreats. "Soul Care Intensives"—guided retreats with spiritual direction—are available for leaders in the ministry and the marketplace.

For more information or for a closer look at our artwork and literature, visit our Web site: www.pottersinn.com.

Or contact us at:

Potter's Inn

6660 Delmonico Drive, Suite D-180

Colorado Springs, CO 80919

Telephone: 719-264-8837

Email: resources@pottersinn.com